500 QUESTIONS AND ANSWERS ON THE BLACK PRESENCE IN THE BIBLE

Published and Distributed by:
Lushena Books
1804-06 West Irving Park Road
Chicago, IL 60613

ISBN 1-930097-19-0

500 QUESTIONS AND ANSWERS ON THE BLACK PRESENCE IN THE BIBLE

Dr. John L. Johnson

(C) 2000 by Dr. John L. Johnson

All rights reserved. No part of this book may be reproduced in any form without written permission from the publishers, except by a reviewer who may quote brief passages in a review to be printed in a newspaper or magazine.

For consistency, use the King James Bible, not the New King James Bible, published in 1979.

First printing April, 2000

Published and Distributed by:
Lushena Books, Inc.
1804 West Irving Park Road
Chicago, IL 60613

Printed in the United States of America

Dedicated to my late mother,
Ida Mae Johnson Cannon,
who encouraged and helped me
to accept "Truth."

ACKNOWLEDGMENTS

I would like to acknowledge Ida M. Bailey, Denise Lott, Dr. James A. Carey, Dr. Theodore Chambers, Ida M. Fanigan, Jeannette Cannon, Artimese Johnson, Julian Ramesses Johnson, Angella Jones, Jerome Miller, Clergyman Frank Mc Phearson, Melvin L. Webb, and Dr. Bailey Williams for their assistance in this publication.

FOREWORD

500 Questions and Answers on the Black Presence in the Bible addresses issues in the Bible from Genesis to Revelation. This book was written so that mankind could become more aware of the African contribution to the Bible, and to abolish the old myth that Black people contributed nothing to the Scriptures. In reality, Africa had a tremendous impact on the early writings of the Bible, from stories and events themselves to those who wrote about them.

This remarkable text is a compilation of questions and answers, geared toward uplifting the minds and spirits of those who are in search of the truth and Salvation. The questions and answers are centered around issues pertaining to the very dawn and fabric of a Black biblical presence.

There has been a universal *trans-mind-formation* by people of color in confronting these issues concerning their heritage. Blacks around the globe, especially those residing in Africa and the Americas, have for centuries faced injustices from Euro-Western missionaries, big business, historians, and politicians, in relation to their overwhelming contribution to both the Bible and natural history.

500 Questions and Answers on the Black Presence in the Bible offers a wealth of biblical and secular information that contradicts many of the myths handed down throughout the centuries about Africa and its people. This book was also assembled to polarize the Bible as one of the oldest documentaries of Black people; reflecting the scriptures' equality of representing all of God's creations, and not just a few.

I am confident that this book will benefit all who search the word of God by offering a broader understanding of the Black presence in the Bible. I pray God's wisdom unto those who read *500 Questions and Answers on the Black Presence in the Bible.*

Author.

St. Louis, Missouri
January, 2000

PREFACE

In October 1996, Dr. Johnson was approached by a group of interesting citizens of the Black community led by Dr. James A. Carey, assistant pastor of Christ Southern Mission Baptist Church, and the Reverend Bailey Williams, president of the Afro-American Men's Club. Dr. Carey requested that Dr. Johnson visit their symposium which was held annually at Missouri University. He insisted that Dr. Johnson attend as the guest speaker and give an introduction to his works, on the presence of Blacks in the Bible and in natural history. Dr. Johnson gladly accepted the offer. The gathering was held on November 4th at 7:00 P.M. at the campus's J.C. Penny Auditorium.

Dr. Johnson, a retired federal employee, received a Bachelor of Science degree from St. Louis University, and a Doctor of Divinity degree from New World Theological Seminary in Texarkana, Arkansas. He served three years in the Marine Corps and one tour in Vietnam. One of his specialties while in Vietnam was speaking the Vietnamese language as a translator. He has spent over twenty-five years intensively researching and highlighting the significance of dark colors, and exposing myths handed down throughout the centuries by the European clergy to Africa, Asia, and the Americas.

Dr. Johnson's published works are: *The Black Biblical Heritage: Four Thousands Years of Black Biblical History, The Lexicon of The Black Biblical Heritage and Secular Terms,* and *God's Kinship With Dark Colors.* These nonfictional books offer a wealth of innovative knowledge about God and creation with relevance to people, places, and things.

Aside from the Old and New Testaments, Dr. Johnson's remarkable works are the first printed materials of their kind to highlight the lineage of Ham, the father of Africa and sections of Asia, along with other Black affiliations to the Bible.

Dr. Johnson has traveled throughout Europe, and portions of Asia and Africa. He has appeared on radio and television programs throughout the country and has received awards for his outstanding writings.

Following his one hour lecture about Africa's contribution to the Bible and natural history, Dr. Johnson then readied himself to be challenged by an exciting audience that was definitely thirsty for the truth. Moments before Dr. Johnson was to encounter the barrage of questions and comments, Dr. Carey calmly instructed the audience to confront the author and speaker with tough questions, while remaining brief, candid, and to the point.

Dr. Carey, given the honor of leading the section, began by asking Dr. Johnson to present a brief description of his book *The Black Biblical Heritage,* in consideration of those who were not present at the beginning of the program.

Dr. Johnson: *The Black Biblical Heritage* is a text that highlights 4000 years of Black biblical history. It is based on the genealogy of man from the creation of Adam, with strong emphasis on the lineage of Noah's youngest son Ham, who was the genetic father of Africa and parts of Asia. The sons of Ham were Cush, Mizraim, Phut, and Canaan, whose descendants can be traced chronologically throughout the Bible. This remarkable book reveals such renowned characters as Adam, the great King and architect Nimrod, the Ethiopian Queen of Sheba, the Canaanite Jezebel, King Solomon, the Black wise men and Madonna, Simon of Cyrene, Simon that was called Niger, Simon the Canaanite, the Messiah, and others. *The Black Biblical Heritage* also reveals many Black priests, prophets, warriors, craftsmen, and teachers, who for centuries discovered and expounded upon many of today's ideas about the universe, religion, government, medicine, and fine arts.

Dr. Carey: Dr. Johnson, what is the significance of history, and why is it critical to Black people?

Dr. Johnson: History is like a universal clock used by people to calculate how we fit on the universal center stage. You see, we're all like a blank sheet of paper waiting to be written upon, whereas mankind, especially Black people, by observing the clock of history, must write and teach their own account, if wishing to compete on an international scale. We must realize that what we write on that blank sheet of paper is what we will become. We as a precessional people must no longer allow our competitors, who view us as incompetent to write and teach that history for us. Either we write it or someone else will, and we may not like what they write. Blacks who have been victimized throughout the globe must understand that a people that seeks knowledge of itself will have to find and nourish that knowledge within itself and not depend upon others who may overlook or discredit it.

Mr. Coolidge: Dr. Johnson, during your introduction you mentioned the Ark uplifting from the continent of Africa to Asia, which you said became man's second home. You also stressed that life and the Garden of Eden originated in Africa. My question is where did you obtain your information to substantiate this claim?

Dr. Johnson: Mr. Coolidge, this information is based upon Genesis 2:11–13, as it describes rivers departing from the Garden of Eden and circling African nations. Hey, lets face it, the Garden of Eden was located within the vicinity of those rivers. It should also be acknowledged that the topaz emerald that Ezekiel mentioned as one of the precious stones of Eden was claimed by Job to have existed in Africa within Ethiopia.

Mr. Coolidge: Where in Ezekiel and Job is such information found?

Dr. Johnson: This information is found in Ezekiel 28:13 and Job 28:19.

Bishop Franklin: Dr. Johnson, I've always believed that life and Eden began in Asia. What new information do you have to convince me otherwise?

Dr. Johnson: Well, before answering your question I would first like to inform you that this information is not new, but an old affidavit that has been systematically kept from the public. The perception that Eden was located in Asia is modernly appealing, but merely rests upon deception and assumption. If there was an Asian Eden, then why weren't the oldest human remains and artifacts discovered in Asia, and not in Africa where there exists overwhelming evidence above and below its soil? Is it not so that Adam and Eve left substantial proof of their entity by producing children, who themselves multiplied for many centuries, before the Global Deluge, and during that period, built homes, fashioned tools, weapons, and utensils, raised livestock, yielded crops, and melted metal? Then why is it that traces of this activity within that period cannot be discovered in Asia, but in Africa? This acknowledgment of Africa being the cradle of mankind is well supported by today's scientists.

Bishop Franklin: That makes a lot of sense. Now could you expound upon the destiny of those Rivers of Eden, especially the Euphrates and Hiddekel, which presently exist in Asia.

Dr. Johnson: Well I would like to first emphasize that ancient Asia was originally called East Africa before being named the Middle East, but that's another subject. However, let me get back to your question. There was a river in Eden that gushed from the soil of Ethiopia and traveled throughout the land to water the Garden. While flowing Northward, it divided into four heads. The first head to depart the gigantic River of Eden was the Pishon which traveled Northwest of Africa. The second head that departed the principal river was the Gihon which later merged with the Pishon. This grand river circled the whole land of Ethiopia, then jet-streamed north of Africa, afterward spilling into the Mediterranean Sea. The name of the third head that flowed from the main river was the Hiddekel which is modernly called the Tigris. This swift and wild river, while flowing from Paradise, apparently plunged underground, flowing hundreds of miles before resurfacing in the Fertile Crescent. From there, it moved southwest, traveling toward the east of Assyria to join the Persian Gulf, earlier called the Ethiopian Sea. The name of the fourth head was the Euphrates. This peaceful river's destination and its departure from the main source of Eden was similar to the Hiddekel's. What I am addressing here, Bishop Franklin, is that the rivers of Eden originated on the continent of Africa, a fact that is confirmed by ancient writers. I would like to also stress that many ancient Jewish scholars were not in agreement with our contemporary belief that the Garden of Eden existed in the Fertile Crescent, or Mesopotamia. The Jewish historian Philo states that Armenia, which is located in Asia, where Eden was said to have existed, was no paradise. He then suggested that Eden was in a remote region, far from his inhabited world, with a river flowing underground, forcing itself through veins in the earth, then emerging in Armenia and elsewhere. The eleventh-century Bible commentator Rashi, commented that the Gihon River which departed from Eden, was the Nile that flowed through Eastern Africa. The great Jewish historian Flavius Josephus agreed by calling the Gihon the African Nile.

Here we observe one Jewish scholar denying Eden's existence in Asia, and the others associating a River of Eden with Africa.1

Pastor Edwards: Dr. Johnson, you stated that the Middle East was first called East Africa. Well, what facts can you produce to support this claim? When was the phrase Middle East first applied?

Dr. Johnson: The answer is very simple if observed from a geographical and domestic observation. You see, in ancient times a portion of what is now called Asia, extending from West China to East Africa, was not called the "Middle East," but "East Africa" or "Ham" by the Negro children of Ham who settled those regions. Let's also remember that the entire Eastern coast of the Mediterranean, before the construction of the Suez Canal, was territorially adjoined to Africa. It was for these reasons that Asia was called "East Africa," before acquiring the name "Middle East." The phrase Middle East was first used by World War II correspondents.

Mrs. Richardson: Dr. Johnson, Israel was called "East Africa?"

Dr. Johnson: Sure. Israel was merely an extended territory of Africa and was called "East Africa," just as Hawaii and Alaska are called "America" or "The United States" even though they have no geographical connection nor any ancient ethnicity with America. However, regardless of this remoteness, we still address the Hawaiians and Alaskans as Caucasians and Americans. Israel was not the only region that was territorially interlocked with Africa. The first inhabitants of the land of Canaan were merely cousins of Africans through Canaan, the brother of Ethiopia, Egypt and Phut, all being the sons of the Negro Ham.

Pastor Edwards: And that's all the proof you have?

Dr. Johnson: What other proof would we need? Ethiopia, the mother of civilization, extended her empire throughout Asia, and the Bible substantiates an Ethiopian presence in those regions. Also, the land of Canaan, which was first dominated by the Negro children of Ham, existed in Asia. The whole continent was named and inhabited by the Negro children of Cush and Canaan.2

Pastor Edwards: Is there any contemporary proof?

Dr. Johnson: Oh my God, mountains of geographical proof. But permit me to only expound upon one. There is a chain of mountains, stretching from Afghanistan to Pakistan, called Hindu-Cush, named after the early inhabitants of the region, the Negro children of Cush!3

Mr. Coolidge: Dr. Johnson, lets go back to the Garden of Eden. What are the translations of the Pishon, Gihon, and Hiddekel Rivers?

Dr. Johnson: The Pishon, which flows from the highlands of Ethiopia, is presently called the Blue Nile. The Gihon, which travels throughout Egypt, is a Greek word for Nile and is modernly called Nile and White Nile. The Hiddekel in Asia is a Persian term meaning Tigris. All four Rivers in ancient times were called "Yam," a term that meant Ham in Old Arabic and also meant Nile, Euphrates, Pacific and Atlantic Ocean, Mediterranean and Red Sea, large river, lake, and rain, along with every known body of water. According to the Greek Herodotus, the Egyptians called the Nile, "Melas," meaning Black or Niger. In Old French, ocean or water was called "Kam," or in Arabic, "Hamy." Biblically, water is a symbol of redemption, everlasting life, and restoration. Two of the longest rivers in Africa are the

Nile and Niger, meaning Black or Negro. The Egyptians worshiped the Nile as a god since the name meant Yam, which was transliterated to "I Am" or "Ham." Remember, the letter "Y" of Yam is interchangeable with "I," thereby altering Yam to Am, I Am, Cam, or Kam, meaning Ham, God, Elo-Him, or Elo-Ham.4

Mr. Jones: Dr. Johnson, why would you call Ethiopia the mother of civilization?

Dr. Johnson: Because Genesis 2:11–12 tells us that Ethiopia and her surrounding districts were the first lands mentioned in the Bible. The Byzantium Stephanus, while commenting on the universal ancient world, spoke of Ethiopia as the first nation on earth. Stephanus went on to say that the Ethiopians were the first people to introduce the worshiping of the Gods and who enacted laws.5

Mrs. Jones: Dr. Johnson, why wasn't Egypt, like Ethiopia, mentioned during the Edenic period?

Dr. Johnson: Because within that age Egypt as a nation didn't exist since the whole region was totally under the Mediterranean Sea. Egypt became part of the continent many centuries later as the Nile flowed down the highlands of Ethiopia, carrying vast quantities of black mud and sediment which gradually elevated that area of the sea to solid ground. That is why the ancient Egyptians referred to Egypt as, "the gift of the Nile." The Roman historian, Pliny, and others, have told interesting stories of islands, stretching hundreds of miles out to sea and becoming part of the mainland in this way.6

Mrs. Jackson: Dr. Johnson, if all territories between Africa and China were called the "East Africa," then what was China called?

Dr. Johnson: It is a fact that China was called the "Far East" and was also occupied by the Negro children of Ham. Diop mentions a Negro empire in Southern China during China's earlier history. In *Les Negritoes*, the black oily-skinned Negroes are said to have once peopled all of South India and China. The *American Anthropologist* says the Japanese and other dark races bear physical traits of Negro descent. The word "China" means "Ham," and to understand this fact, one must first realize that the ancient letter "N" was interchangeable with "M," therefore altering China to "Chima," or "Chama," which is the same as Cham, Hima, Hama, or Ham.7

Mrs. Jackson: Dr. Johnson, how would you define a fact?

Dr. Johnson: Something that has been researched and has been proven to be true.

Brother Tidwell: Dr. Johnson, you stated that the Euphrates and the Hiddekel Rivers traveled from Africa to Asia underground. How did you come to this belief? I find it quite difficult to believe.

Dr. Johnson: Brother Tidwell, let me first inform you that this information I am offering is not a figment of my imagination, but knowledge based upon mountains of evidence. For instance, in Mammoth Cave, located in Kentucky, there exist two rivers flowing underground. The cave also contains lakes and waterfalls.8

Mr. Jones: Interesting. But, Dr. Johnson, can you produce other evidence that will convince me, as a skeptic, that the Euphrates and Hiddekel Rivers flowed from Africa underground?

Dr. Johnson: As I have commented earlier, this information is based upon ancient documentation. The Greek, Philostratus, states that the Armenians and the Arabs of his epoch were convinced that the Euphrates River flowed to Africa underground, then mingled with the Nile. Higgins says that the Euphrates was called the Nile, and traveled beneath the surface. The Egyptologist, James Henry Breasted, states that the Eastern Mediterranean once flowed into the Euphrates, causing the Euphrates to spill into the Nile Delta. Hall says that the Egyptians called the Euphrates the Nile, and that it flowed south. Now, it's obvious that the Hiddekel, which is modernly called the Tigris, had a similar traveling route. The Greek historian and geographer, Strabo, compared the Tigris with the Syrian Arontes River, which plunged underground for a considerable distance and resurfaced. Last, but not least, the Roman historian Pliny says that the Tigris River would end its source near the mountains of Taurus, sinking underground and resurfacing on the other side of Nymphaeum. The name Tigris, anciently, meant black!9

Mr. Jackson: Very well expressed, Dr. Johnson, but I still find it difficult to conceive of the Hiddekel and Euphrates jet-streaming out of Africa to Asia, because I personally can't find any point of evidence to support that belief."

Dr. Johnson: Mr. Jackson, what evidence are you searching for?

Mr. Jackson: Well, to actually witness these rivers flowing from, or to Africa.

Dr. Johnson: Mr. Jackson, a lot is going on around us that we can't see, but can only be believed by faith and scientific proof. Remember, in ancient times man's eyes misled him to believe the sun circled the earth. He also believed the earth was flat because he couldn't see around it! Mr. Jackson, people can't depend solely upon their eyes to unravel the mysteries of the universe. Now, in reference to the four Rivers of Eden, I believe the Scriptures when describing these rivers as deriving from one source which clearly indicates both an above and below ground connection.

This biblical acknowledgment, along with the historical account of the Greek Philostratus (170–245 B.C.), who spoke of an underground connection between the Euphrates and the Nile, should eliminate further doubt. Our prime concern should be focused around the very origin of these rivers, rather than with present appearances.

Mr. Jackson: Why should it eliminate further doubt?

Dr. Johnson: Mr. Jackson, look at it from a different perspective. If the Bible describes the four rivers as deriving from one source, and then over 2500 years later the Negro Babylonians spoke of these same rivers as interlocking, this should definitely eliminate one's doubt. The Greek Philostratus (170–245 B.C.), recorded the same event 1500 years later, by documenting that the Euphrates and the Nile merged through an underground channel. This recognition should reinforce the belief that those rivers continued to merge from the time of their creation until Philostratus' era. What could possibly prevent these rivers from continuing this same natural event for another 1700 years until modern times?

Higgins (1773–1833), who lived about 1600 years after Philostratus, recorded that the Euphrates was said to be the Nile, and was connected to Africa through an underground channel. It was 97 years later that Hall (1873–1930) wrote that the Egyptians, who were one of the world's earliest civilizations, called the Euphrates the Nile.

Elder Benson: Dr. Johnson, you had mentioned Africa as being the cradle of mankind. Does that include Adam and Eve, and if so, what race and color were they?

Dr. Johnson: Adam and Eve were a black-skinned couple who were created in the tropic zone, an area that produces the black/brown colored skin. The couple never identified themselves racially, but rather adhered to Adamites or children of God. Historians called them "Antediluvians," meaning "people before the flood." Even though the pair never linked themselves to a race, it should be acknowledged that the Negro's feature or physical structure was embodied in their appearances during the Antediluvian period. The earliest inhabitants of ancient Africa and Asia possessed a Negroid description. I would like to also interject that anthropologists such as Dr. Leaky are in congruence with the Bible that the first man resided in a tropical environment, and that the tropics only produce black and brown people.

The Greek Herodotus plainly stated that the people of India and Mesopotamia were black-skinned. He addressed them as black Ethiopians. The historian Rogers says that the inhabitant of a tropical region is never white. This information is not difficult to understand by those who study and have the power of the Holy Spirit.10

Brother Tidwell: Dr. Johnson, where in the Bible does it comment on Adam and Eve living in the tropics, and, again, how do you know they were black looking?

Dr. Johnson: The Bible doesn't use the words "tropic" and "black," but does indicate them by describing the Rivers of Eden as circling Black-African nations, which exist in the tropics. Adam and Eve walked around naked and had all the fruits of the world, such as pineapples, bananas, and many others that could not have grown in a cold climate.11

Elder Benson: Dr. Johnson, how do you know that Adam and Eve were black-skinned people, and favored the Negro race?

Mrs. Jackson: Good question because I always believed Eve to be a White woman because she was made from a white rib.

Dr. Johnson: I do not mean to be repetitious, but if my earlier answer didn't convince you, then allow me to approach the question from a different angle by reminding you that Jesus Ham-Ashiah, or Messiah, is described as having hair like pure wool, and arms and feet the color of fine brass, as if burned in a furnace. Jesus Ham-Ashiah, or Messiah, is also described as possessing the color of a dark jasper and sardine stone, as well as being identified as the second Adam. St. John's description of Jesus Ham-Ashiah, or Messiah, clearly portrays a dark-skinned, woolly headed man. If Jesus Ham-Ashiah, or Messiah, was labeled the second Adam, then wouldn't Adam have favored Him? Adam was created in the image of God, by which Daniel described as having a human figure with pure wool hair and dark skin. I would also like to remind you that *Newsweek* illustrated Adam and Eve as Blacks. Now, to your comment Mrs. Jackson, I hope you'll never forget that the white rib Eve was made from, was taken from the body of a Black man. Face it, Mrs. Jackson, reality is better than fiction.12

Mr. Higgins: Dr. Johnson, why do you repeatedly address Jesus as Jesus Ham-Ashiah?

Dr. Johnson: Because Ham-Ashiah, Ham-Masiah, Ham-Elehk, Ham-Ahiah, Ham-Massiah, or Ham-Melek is the Hebrew root word for Messiah; a truth that most preachers or missionaries will choke with a smile before admitting! Throughout this section I will apply various Hebrew names for the "Supreme Creator" and "Jesus the Savior." Remember, the Hebrews had numerous names for God.13

Mrs. Pinkham: Dr. Johnson, I believe that Jesus had a color, but can we actually say that His skin was extremely black?

Dr. Johnson: Heavenly yes, since the Scriptures mention His arms and feet as if burned in a furnace. Mrs. Pinkham, I am sure that you know what burned toast or bacon looks like? Jesus' skin is also associated with brass or bronze, the same as copper, since brass or bronze is made from copper. *Webster's Third New International Dictionary* identifies a black copper called "melaconite." The historian Bunsen says that the Egyptians called copper or bronze, "Kam," which is the same as Black or Ham! Budge was in agreement.14

Ms. Dupree: Dr. Johnson, could Jesus have been dark or black skinned, but not a Black man or Negro?

Dr. Johnson: Absolutely not, don't forget that Jesus Ham-Ashiah or Messiah, in addition to having black skin, possessed a pure-wool hair texture that is only found among Negroes, or among those of Negro descent. If a person has black skin, then he or she is certainly a Negro. Remember, the color black is defined as "Nigger" or "Negro," and to believe that a person can have black skin without being a Negro is totally absurd! For once in your life, audience, believe what your eyes see. It is idiotic to stand near a sooty-skinned foreigner and think that his deep black skin has no association to Africa or Black America. We may object to calling dark-skinned foreigners Negroes, but if their skin is black, then so are they regardless of their culture.

The tragedy is that the Black man has been trained to manipulate his own mind to exclude this truth from his conscience. How sad that when Blacks are in the vicinity of a dark or black-skinned counterpart from abroad, they critically error in noticing their own genetic blueprint in that very person. I must sincerely say that when it comes to brainwashing, the slavemaster truly did his job well.

Mrs. Pinkham: But Jesus was a Jew!

Dr. Johnson: True, by nationality or culture, He was a Jew, but through genealogy He was none other than a Black man. That's why the KKK and other radical groups hate Jews and Blacks, because they know that the two are merely a blend of one race; the Negro race. The antiquarians such as Celsus, Plutarch, Tacitus, Eusebius, and Diodorus, all agreed that the original Hebrews were Ethiopians and Egyptians who were forced out of Egypt. According to M. Fishberg in the *American Anthropologist,* the biblical Cushite were Negroes with whom the Jews freely mingled. Fishberg went on to say that the ancient Hebrews possessed largely Negro features such as woolly hair, dark skin, thick lips that folded, large heads, and projecting jaws. Jesus Ham-Ashiah, or Messiah, was a descendant of those people. Remember, according to the prophets Zephaniah and Amos, the ancient Jews lived throughout Africa. This information is not difficult to understand by those who study and have the power of the Holy Spirit.15

Ms. Louis: Dr. Johnson, where else in the Bible does it mention Jews and Ethiopians intermingling?

Dr. Johnson: Try Numbers 12:1 where it speaks of Moses' Negro wife Zipporah, who was Ethiopian or of the Negro race. The couple had two biracial sons, Gershom and Eliezer. Here we notice Moses, the founding father of the Hebrew Bible, promoting interracial marriage with God's approval.

Mrs. Richardson: Dr. Johnson, isn't Jesus part of every man?

Dr. Johnson: Sure He is, but He couldn't have been a White man with woolly hair and dark skin.16

Sister Ford: Dr. Johnson, I've always believed Jesus to have favored an Indian or a Mohammedan. What do you think?

Dr. Johnson: Totally preposterous, since I've never seen an Indian or an Arab with pure wool hair!

Mr. Jones: Dr. Johnson, If Adam was a black-skinned man, then why is his name defined as "red?"

Dr. Johnson: I would like to first advise you, Mr. Jones, that according to Hastings, Jones, and Bryant, the name Adam was originally spelled "Adham," meaning Homo, Man, and Ham, which is a transliteration of God-Ham, since "Ad" of Adham means God, and naturally "Ham" indicates the color black. My objective is to expose the name Adam as a word meaning black. Even if we avoid the original spelling, Adham, in reference to Adam, the name would still mean God-Ham or God-Black, since according to Dr. William Smith and Professor Charles Horne, "Am" of Adam is equivalent to Ham. Adam is also defined as "dark red earth," "reddish brown and black." Now answering your question of why Adam is defined as red will largely depend upon your acceptance that red is equivalent to black. Let me give you an example. When blood is caught in a vessel, it becomes cool, afterward drying up and leaving a brownish-black solid mass or clot. However, if you move that scab, solid mass, or clot to a moist environment, or water, that same black scab, through maceration, will turn red again.17

Mrs. Pinkham: Dr. Johnson, Daniel 7:9 doesn't say that Jesus' hair was pure wool, but like pure wool, meaning it wasn't the same as wool, but like wool.

Dr. Johnson: Mrs. Pinkham, the word "like" means equal, equivalent, or the same; search your dictionary.

Mr. Jones: Dr. Johnson, I can't believe that Jesus' skin was extremely black, could you expound more on the subject?

Dr. Johnson: Mr. Jones, the hair on your head is woolly, but not of pure texture. I grasp this detection based upon your bright complexion, and upon the fact that the average American Black, including myself, whose lineage can be traced back to slavery, has about 25% Caucasian blood in his veins. The only people on earth to possess a pure wool texture are those living in Africa, such as the Pygmies, Nigerians, the Zulu people, and others. Now my point is to make you aware of the fact that it appears that only a black-skinned person of the Negro race can produce a pure wool texture, where the light-skinned people, including the light-skinned Negroes, can't. I would also like to stress that Jesus Ham-Ashiah, or Messiah, lived along the Mediterranean coast; an area of people of color.18

Mr. Gibbes: Dr. Johnson, if Black peoples' hair is said to be bad hair, then why do the Scriptures identify the Messianic King, or Jesus Christ, as having pure wool hair?

Dr. Johnson: Because wool hair was anciently viewed as sacred or holy. In most modern icons, the hair of Jesus Ham-Ashiah, or Messiah, along with other features have been distorted from woolly to straight, and from broad to keen. However, the sheep or lamb is still presented in some of those fake Euro-portraits of Jesus, with its sacred woolly hair!

Mr. Gibbes: What makes you think that wool hair represented sacredness?

Dr. Johnson: In Daniel 7:9, and Revelation 1:14–15, wool hair is a description of God-Hama-Kom and His Son. Would the Supreme Creator and His Son possess an inferior description? In Song of Solomon 5:11, the Colored King Solomon, who was the wisest man to ever live, also possessed a rough wool texture.

Ms. Dupree: Dr. Johnson, why would you address God, as "God-Hama-Kom?"

Dr. Johnson: Because that's what the Hebrews called Him, and keep in mind that the name Ham was also called Hama. The suffix "Kom" of God-Hama-Kom is also called Hom or Ham, since the ancient letter "K" was exchanged for "H." I would like to also stress, that God-Hama-Kom was always addressed with titles referring to darkness.

El Shaddai and Elohim are merely terms meaning black or dark. The word "Shad" of El Shaddai is a synonym for shade, shadow, dark, and black, whereas "Dai" of El Shaddai is merely an another expression for day, since the letter "I" is exchanged for "Y." Keep in mind that the first day was evening and morning, which indicated darkness! The Hebrews also called God-Hama-Kom "Mah," which in reverse is spelled "Ham." Remember, the Hebrews were obsessed with applying anagrams. An anagram is created when the letters of a phrase or word are rearranged, or when a word is spelled backward. The word "Elohim" is equivalent to "Elo-Ham," since the ancient letter "I" was exchanged for "A." Naturally the name Ham meant black. God-Hama-Kom is an enigma or mystery; the Greek word for enigma is "darkly!"[19]

Mr. Jones: Dr. Johnson, my Bible says that Solomon had bushy hair, not woolly hair.

Dr. Johnson: I'm aware, but the synonym for bushy is woolly![20]

Mrs. Richardson: Dr. Johnson, if Blacks have 25% Caucasian blood, then how much Black blood do Caucasians have?

Dr. Johnson: The last survey said 5%. Let me also comment that Weisgerber says that the whitest people living in Northern Africa are mixed with Negro blood. Last, but not least, I'm sure we are all aware of The Red Cross and blood banks? Isn't the Negro blood issued throughout the world to various ethnic groups and races? Believe me Mrs. Richardson, there is some African in us all.21

Mr. Coolidge: Dr. Johnson, the encyclopedia says that the Euphrates, from a modern observation, receives its main source of water from the rains flowing down the mountains of Armenia. Now how does this constitute the underground channels?

Dr. Johnson: Mr. Coolidge, the encyclopedia is somewhat correct, but not thorough. Remember, it didn't rain during the Antediluvian period, which covered a timespan of some 1700 years. These rivers were highly active in movement, and yet only received vast rains during and after the Great Flood. Once again, Mr. Coolidge, prior to the flood, these rivers, from Adam to Noah, were originally sourced from an underground channel, long before man had any perception of rain.

Mr. Coolidge: What you're saying makes a lot of sense. My next question is why haven't theologians or church biblicists expounded on this subject?

Dr. Johnson: For several reasons; but let me first say that many scientists have always known this, but have only shared the greater bulk of this knowledge with their peers. The clergy has also realized this information, but fears teaching it, saying it doesn't blend in with church doctrine. Let's face it; there are certain secrets concerning our ancient religion and the Bible that are modernly covered up, for fear that it will destabalize or undermine Europe's ethnocentrism, especially concerning Eden's true location.

Sister Ford: Dr. Johnson, can you explain why the subject of these rivers is important?

Dr. Johnson: For the simple reason that these rivers have a direct connection to Africa, Adam, and the Garden of Eden.

Mrs. Jefferson: Dr. Johnson, Genesis 2:11 speaks of the first river circling Havilah. My concern is that there were two Havilahs; a Hamitic and Semitic Havilah. Now which Havilah did the Pishon River circle?

Dr. Johnson: It was the Hamitic Havilah that existed about seven generations before the Semitic Havilah. The Hamitic Havilah was the Son of Cush who lived about 280 years prior to the Semitic Havilah, who was the son of Joktan. Keep in mind that a generation during the dawn of man's history was not 20 years but 40 since man lived longer during that age. Don't forget that Mathusala lived to be 969 years old.

Mr. Jackson: Dr. Johnson where is the Hamitic Havilah presently located, and what does the name modernly fall under?

Dr. Johnson: In East Africa, which is now called "The Middle East," Havilah is modernly called "Somaliland," "Djibouti," or "The Horn of Africa."

Mr. Jackson: I see, but do scholars confirm this fact?

Dr. Johnson: The Roman historian Pliny, the Jewish Aharoni, and the Black American Rudolph Windsor, among other sources, have illustrated and commented that Havilah was located in East Africa.[22]

Mr. Coolidge: Dr. Johnson, in 1977 the oldest human remains were found in Ethiopia, Africa. The body was that of a woman whom scientists named "Lucy" and dubbed "the mother of mankind." Why is the African woman called the origin of the human race, without mentioning the man? What's your comment?

Dr. Johnson: Mr. Coolidge let us not overlook that the first woman was made from the rib of man, which plainly indicates that man was first.

Mr. Jackson: Can science and religion mix?

Dr. Johnson: Absolutely. There are biblical and non-biblical archaeologists who agree and disagree. For example, both groups agree that a flood once occurred; fragments of Noah's Ark are literally strewn between Turkey and Russia; and a man called Jesus was crucified in Palestine. However, they equally disagree on how life began, the natural versus the supernatural, and the origin of time.

Strange to say, there is a Jewish sect called the Hallel who believe (as do many archaeologists) that man evolved through the process of evolution, from a tiny one-cell organism called the ameba. They believe this process was part God's original blueprint.

Mrs. Pinkham: Dr. Johnson, do you really believe that science and religion mix? I don't believe in science.

Dr. Johnson: Yes, I do believe. Abraham, Isaac and Solomon practiced science. Abraham was a geologist, which helped him to detect water beneath the surface by which he built wells. According to I Kings 4:29–33, Solomon with his many gifts would be modernly defined as a botanist, ornithologist, and zoolologist. Mrs. Pinkham, if you don't believe in science then stop driving your automobile, get rid of your wrist watch, stop watching television, flying in jets, and eating peanut butter.

Elder Benson: Dr. Johnson, what color was Noah and how do you know?

Dr. Johnson: Remember, Noah had a black son named Ham. The biology law says that white can not produce black, but only in reverse. Now how could Noah have fathered Ham had Noah not been black himself? Not only were Noah and Ham black, but also Shem and Japhite.

Elder Benson: You're saying Shem and Japheth were black in color? Be more thorough.

Dr. Johnson: Well, let's first begin with the Semitic Hebrews. From Shem up to the reign Solomon, Semites were a black-skinned people. It was just following the death of Solomon that the Semitic people began to change from black to white. Now, concerning Japheth, the Scriptures doesn't give an account of his whiteness, but merely informs us of what turns a black skin white! Biblically, this information is found in Exodus 4:6–7; Numbers 12:10; the 13th chapter of Leviticus, and II Kings 5:27. I would like to also emphasize that the bitter friction between the Black, Semite and White, is largely triggered by the fact that Semitic and Caucasian people, have lost their original Adamic color; an acknowledgment that has caused Semites and Whites to culturally apply reverse psychology tactics regarding the Negro's complexion.

Elder Benson: So you're saying that before the Deluge and dispersal of Babel, both Shem and Japheth were black-skinned?

Dr. Johnson: That is totally correct. Shem and Japheth evacuated the Tower of Babel as black-skinned individuals. It has been proven many times that a black-skinned race first occupied all of Europe before the presence of Whites! There is no evidence of a White race originating on any continent other than Europe, which clearly indicates that the White race originated out of the indigenous darker race. Jean Finot says that the White race, the ethnic pride of Europe, is only a direct fruit of the Negro race. Isaac

Taylor says that the skeleton of the Cro-Magnon matched that of the Negro more than any skeleton discovered on the European Continent. Ellen Churchill says the long-headed people of Northern Europe were a Mediterranean race of African origin with brunette hair that bleached out under the sun of the Scandinavian skies. Sir Harry H. Johnston commented that many thousand years ago, a Negroid race had penetrated Europe through Italy and France, leaving traces in the present day in the people of Southern Italy, Sicily, Sardina, Southern and Western France, and even in the United Kingdom of Great Britain and Ireland.23

Mrs. Lott: Dr. Johnson, are you saying that in the beginning the White man or race didn't exist?

Dr. Johnson: Scripturally, what we call a White man has always existed biologically, but not physically until following the death of Solomon. Biblically, this information is found in Exodus 4:6–7; Numbers 12:10; the 13th chapter of Leviticus, and II Kings 5:27.

Mrs. Jackson: Dr. Johnson what available sources verify your claim, and how can a Black produce a White? Your comment sounds preposterous!

Dr. Johnson: You can verify this information in the U.S. News, September 16, 1991, and many other old documents, such as *The Mediterranean Races* by the Italian Sergi, who called the Europeans "Africans." To your second question, the blackest of Blacks can produce the whitest of White. Have you overlooked the fact that Negroes can produce albinos?24

Mr. Jackson: Yes but Whites also produces albinos!

Dr. Johnson: Sure, but Whites cannot produce the color black.

Mrs. Pinkham: I've seen Whites produce the color black!

Dr. Johnson: Impossible. They may have looked physically white, but genetically they were Blacks passing as Whites.

Mr. Jackson: Dr. Johnson are you advocating race and pride, or may I say that "black thing?"

Dr. Johnson: Oh no, just grace and the spirit of God-Hama-Kom. Mr. Jackson I wasn't invited here to comment on that "black thing," but that "truth thing!" My fellow brethren, a Christian will never hide the truth based upon color or prejudice. My purpose here is not to promote color, but to promote the truth which just so happens to be about color.

Mrs. Pinkham: Dr. Johnson, since all things are possible with God, couldn't He have allowed a White man to produce a Black man?

Dr. Johnson: It's true that all things are possible with God-Eloham. However, it is also true that God-Yahwe has a fixed law of the universe that He will never alter during His encounter with man. One of these laws happens to be that white can not produce black. Sure, all things are possible with Him, but God-Eloham will never allow a person to fly in the same manner as our mythical superman, or have the power to stare at an object with super laser-beam eyes that melt steel, or be a man who can bend solid bars with his bare hands. Again, all things are possible with God-Eloham, yet He will never create a person of this magnitude.

God-Eloham can instantly alter the sun to rotate around the earth, but instead has chosen to maintain His original law of the universe. It is possible that God-Eloham could redesign man to run up to the speed of 300 miles-per-hour, but once again, He has chosen to maintain man's natural state, by sustaining an unchangeable law of the universe.

Another set law of God's universe is that the greatest of greatest comes out of darkness. In Genesis 1:1–3, God-Eloham thrust Himself out of darkness saying let there be light. He went on to emphasize in Isaiah 45:3 that darkness embodies valuable treasures. In Luke 2:7–8; 23:44, and John 20:1–3, Jesus Ham-Ashiah, or Messiah, was born at night, crucified during daylight and resurrected in the dark. Last, but not least, every human being is conceived and developed in their mother's womb, which is pitch black dark!

Elder Peterson: Dr. Johnson, most of us are familiar with the term Elohim as another Hebrew expression for God-Yahwe. I've noticed your pronunciation and spelling of this word, as Eloham instead of Elohim. Why?

Dr. Johnson: Good question, because Elohim can be pronounced and spelled Eloham, Elohum, Elohem, Elohom, or Elohym, since all vowels are interchangeable. *The Oxford English Dictionary* translates "Him" as Ham, Hem, Hom, Hum, and Hym. I will throughout this program spell and pronounce Elohim as "Eloham," which clearly indicates "Ham!" Naturally, "Elo" of Elohim, is the same as Eli meaning God, constituting Elohim as God-Ham.

Dr. Carey: Dr. Johnson in your introduction you seem to give Ham and his four sons, Ethiopia, Egypt, Phut, and Canaan, a tremendous amount of praises and honors. Why do you see Ham and his children as the true heroes of the Bible?

Dr. Johnson: I would first like to reiterate that in Genesis 2:11–12, the first nations mentioned in the Scriptures were the nations of Ham. In Genesis 14:5; I Chronicles 4:40; Psalm 105:23–27, and 106:19–23, the name of Ham alone (of Noah's three sons) was given to lands or nations. Following the Deluge, it was Ham's grandson, Nimrod, who formed the world's first sophisticated government in Babylon, and became its "nigid" or ruler. It was this same architectural and ingenious Nimrod who built the world's first skyscraper, known then as the Tower of Babel, which was none other than a ziggurate pyramid.

After the dispersal of Babel, Ethiopia, Egypt, Phut, and Canaan, who were children of Ham, developed the high-cultured systems of the ancient world. Professor Seignobos states that religion and government (as well as the skills of sculpture, writing, painting, weaving cloths, working metals, and cultivating the soil) were developed by the Negroes while the Jews, Persians, Greeks, Romans and Hindus were in a savage state. Rawlingson says that Egypt, Babylon, Mizraim, and Nimrod were descendants of Ham, and led the way and acted as pioneers of mankind in the various untrodden fields of art, literature, science, alphabetic writing, astronomy, history, chronology, architecture, plastic art, sculpture, navigation, agriculture, and textiles.

From a religious perspective, Ham, Adam, and Jesus Ham-Ashiah, or Messiah, were the three most influential men to walk this earth. It was these three key figures who laid the cornerstone for man and civilization. Jesus Ham-Ashiah, or Messiah, who is the second Adam, also represents God the Ad, the same as Father and Am, the same as Ham. Remember, the two words Ad and Am, if merged, means Adam or Adham.

In Exodus 3:13–14 and John 8:58, God and the Son identify themselves as I Am, meaning Am, Ham, Cam, or Cham. The name Ham also signifies philosophy, mathematical sciences, and the world's first government called Hamacracy!

My point, Dr. Carey, is to alert the audience to realize that the names Ham, Adam or Adham, and Jesus Ham-Ashiah, or

Messiah, are a contraction of only one name, meaning Yahwe or Jehova. The name Ham was praised in ancient times, and was viewed as Divine! The Ethiopians and Egyptians called their father Ham, "Amen," or "Amen-Ra." The Hebrews postured the name Ham as a suffix of Elohim or Eloham, since the Hebrew letter "I," was interchangeable with "A," thereby altering Elohim to Eloham. The ancients also called Elohim, I Am, the same as Ham or Amen, since the Semitic letter "I" was exchanged for "C" (Ch), the "C" (Ch) for "K" (Kh), and the "K" (Kh) for "H," thereby altering I Am to "Cam," the French word for Ham; "Cham," the Hebrew and Latin expression for Ham; "Kam," a Dutch term for Ham; and "Ham," an English expression.

The Hebrews also called Yahwe, "Ham-A-Kom." The name Ham was later used as a suffix to the word Abraham; an infix to Has-Ham-Ma-Im, which is another Hebrew word for God-Elohim or God-Eloham, and a prefix of the Hebrew word "Ham-Melech," Ham-Elkh," "Ham-Ashiah" or "Ham-Mashiah," meaning Amen, Jesus Ham-Ashiah or Messiah, King or Anointed, long before the physical presence of Abraham and Jesus Ham-Ashiah or Messiah!

The transliteration of the name Ham was universally linked to all ancient deities. Remember, the Ethiopians, Egyptians and other nations, throughout the centuries, addressed Ham as Amen, Ra, Ra-Amen, Ra-Ham, Osiris, Ptah, No, Nu, Serapis, Baal, Yahwe-Elohim, Ng, Nga, Nego, Niger, Negus, Cneph, the same as Christna, Khnum, Khnum-Ra, etc. Every name rendered to Egypt's Supreme Deity, was none other than a synonymic form of Ham!

The Greeks worshiped Ham's oldest son, Cush, as "Apollo," his grandson, Nimrod, as "Hercules," the Ethiopian Queen of Sheba, "Diana" or "Artemis," and Ham himself, as "Zeus," the Supreme Creator. The Romans called Ham, "Jupiter." The Canaanites addressed Ham as Baal or Baal-Ham-On, the same as On or Heliopolis, the City of the Sun or Ham, whereas the Moabites called Ham "Chemosh." The Deity Bamoth-Baal and other Baals, who were styled as Ham, were called "Zeus" by the Greeks. The Greek's obsession with worshiping Ham and his sons has led many historians to shrewdly label the ancient Greek religion as mythical, since its roots were centered upon deifying the Negro gender.

The Heavenly father, Jehova, was called Ham or Baal by the Black Hebrews and Canaanites. They addressed Him, as Elohim, same as Elo-Ham, meaning God-Ham. The term "El" or "Elo" of Elohim means God, whereas, Him is equivalent to Ham, since both letters "A" and "I" are interchangeable, meaning God. My fellow brethren, the topic concerning Ham is endless!25

Elder Petterson: Why would you say endless?

Dr. Johnson: Well as previously stated, the name Ham means God-Yehwe, since the letter "H" of Ham is equal to "K," the "K" to "C," the "C" to the letter "I," which in turn alters the word "Ham" to "I Am," which is endless! All words, sounds, and every conceivable thought, can be traced to one common origin; Ham or I Am, which is God-Yahwe. This awareness has disturbed modern scholars and they have tried to show abnormality by distorting the name Ham in various literature and new translations to indicate a curse or inferiority.

Reverend Pierce: Dr. Johnson, I personally view the Hebrews as the heroes of the Bible since they were the people from whom came the Messiah Christ.

Dr. Johnson: I agree to a certain extent. Remember, sir, that before Abraham was born, Ethiopia, Egypt, Phut, and Canaan existed as great nations. They recognized and worshiped Jesus

Ham-Ashiah, or Messiah, 2000 years before His birth, and long before Abraham became the father of the Hebrews. We must also remember that the Hebrew people were merely an offshoot of the Negro race, a fact that is evidenced throughout the Bible. That is why most theologians have falsely identified the Negro Canaanites as Semitics in order to cover up the Black link among the Negroes and Hebrews who were a blend of one race. My point, sir, is that Christ Himself was a Negro!

The Roman historian Tacitus clearly recorded that when Jews entered Rome, most Romans mistook them as Ethiopians. Fishberg says that the ancient Hebrews possessed largely Negro features such as woolly hair, dark skin, thick lips that folded, large heads, and projecting jaws. Remember, according to the prophets Amos and Zephaniah, the ancient Jews lived in Ethiopia. Godbey spoke of Jews living throughout Africa. This information is not difficult to understand by those who study and have the power of the Holy Spirit.26

Reverend Pierce: My point, Dr. Johnson, is that the Hebrews were called God's people.

Dr. Johnson: The Bible's point, sir, is that the Negroes were also called God-Yahwe's people in Isaiah 19:22–25. Keep in mind that during that period Egypt was ruled by the 25th Ethiopian Dynasty. These rulers were extremely black!

Bishop Franklin: Brethren, not only were the Negroes called God's people, but they were the first to attain this title. Dr. Johnson can you elaborate more on that topic?

Dr. Johnson: The Negro Ethiopian and Egyptians were a great people having the acknowledgment of one God and the coming of the Messiah long before Abraham or the Israelite nation existed. These Negro worshipers for many centuries were addressed by Yahwe-Eloham, as "My people." Eloham's close relationship with the Negro family of nations can be observed as far back as Nimrod the giant, whose genealogy can be traced to Cush, Ham, Noah and Adham or Adam.

Nimrod was called the mighty hunter before Yehwe-Eloham, and like many of Eloham's favorites, Nimrod became a victim of defiance which, in turn, caused a gradual disassociation between the Negro race and Eloham. The Negro Egyptians, who were students of their Negro cousins the Ethiopians, shared a similar experience. The Ethiopian and Egyptian's opposition to Eloham motivated Him to show favor toward Abram who lived among the Negro Ethiopians, or Chaldees, in Ur. Abram, who once worshiped Negro Deities, seemed to have found favor in Eloham's eyes by becoming humble.

The Negro Ethiopians and Egyptians having once faithfully served Yahwe-Eloham to their highest endeavor, suddenly found themselves in defiance, which cost them the loss of their Divine status-inheritance which the house of Abraham inherited. It was the disobedience of Ethiopia and Egypt that constituted Israel as Eloham's inheritance. God-Eloham assured Israel that He gave up the Negro nations of Ethiopia, Egypt and Seba as ransom for them; the same exemplification He initiated by giving up his only begotten Son, Jesus Christ, as a ransom for mankind.27

Mrs. Pinkham: Dr. Johnson, are you saying that God favored the Black man over the White man?

Dr. Johnson: No, but He did give the Negro race, which was Ethiopia, Egypt, Phut and Canaan, the gift of knowledge which they passed on to others, thereby making us all equal in His eyes.

Mr. Jones: Dr. Johnson what sources reveal that the letters "K," "C" and "I" are interchangeable?

Dr. Johnson: That information is found in *The Oxford English Dictionary* and *An Introduction to the Comparative Grammar of the Semitic Languages* by Moscati.

Mr. Jones: I am convinced that the letter "K" is exchanged for "C," because my little sister, Katherine, sometimes uses both letters to spell her name, but the letter "I" is something I'll have to look further into.

Brother Hightower: Dr. Johnson, ever since I was a child the clergy has always emphasized that the name Ham represented a curse. I have personally searched the Scriptures and have never found any evidence to support their claim. What are your comment?

Dr. Johnson: Brother Hightower, this old lie which never existed in Scripture, was handed down by the Euro-clergy to our early, illiterate Black ministers who still to this day teach that same old fairy tale. The tragedy is that most ministers never took the time to research the story, and don't realize that Genesis 9:25 mentions nothing about Ham's skin changing color. To the contrary, every curse referred to in the Bible in reference to skin color, states that the cursed ones were turned white. The Euro-clergy has practiced reverse psychology by teaching the opposite. They have taught this lie about Ham with such vigor and consistency, that it appears they have even convinced themselves of it. In fact, Miriam, Naaman, Gehazi, Uzziah, and the hand of Moses were all turned white as a result of a curse. Therefore, it could not be more obvious that they were originally black.

Brother Hightower: Dr. Johnson, to imply that the name Ham represents a curse would also infer that God's name is cursed if the name Ham is a synonym to "I Am" or "Cham."[28]

Dr. Johnson: Your comments are well taken. World scholars have always used double talk by crediting Egypt as the world's greatest of the greatest. But they will turn right around and preach that Ham represents a curse. How contradicting, since the term "Egypt" itself is a Greek translation of the word "Ham" or "Kam!"

Scholars say the name Ham represents a curse, yet in Isaiah 19:25 God blessed the name of Ham by saying, bless be Egypt my people. Remember, the term "Egypt" means Ham or Kam, which in turn means Black. Let me also stress that most Euro-scholars play on the public intelligence by juggling conceptions. For example, many will say that Ethiopians live in Africa but aren't Negroes. How misleading, since the word "Ethiopia" itself means Black or Negro!

Sister Payne: So you're saying that Ham and his descendants were blessed?

Dr. Johnson: Sure. In Genesis 9:1, God-Eloham, or Elohim, blessed Ham as he departed the Ark.

Mr. Coolidge: My goodness, Dr. Johnson, why do you think we've overlooked these key points?

Dr. Johnson: For several reasons. One reason is our own lack of interest in exploring the subject. Again, some Black ministers have seriously failed to alert their congregations to these facts. Also, the Euro-translators, while translating the Bible, had a tendency to avoid describing people, places, and things, in relation to Blacks. Mr. Coolidge, when a person goes shopping, they often come home with only what they were in search of. It is likely that a person will not discover what they don't know exists. We must also remember that it has been instilled in Black people to deny a Negro presence in the Bible.

Mrs. Jackson: Dr. Johnson, you said that the name Ham meant "black." Well, in my Bible dictionary it says "Hot," and not "black."

Dr. Johnson: Mrs. Jackson, you're right. The name Ham represents Hot and every other conceivable thought, since it is equivalent to "I Am," which is everything! However, let me refocus on the word "Hot." Geographically, Ham was called Hot because of the hot climate he and his offspring endured. Genetically, Ham was called Black because of his extreme black skin. Spiritually, Ham was given so many other titles that I really wouldn't attempt to name them all. The Ethiopians called him Amen and Ra; the Egyptians, who learned their culture from the Ethiopians, also called him Amen, Ra, and many other names (Amon-Ra, Osiris, Horus, etc.); the Hebrews used his name as a suffix to their God Elo-Him or Elo-Ham; the Canaanite called him Baal or Baal-Hamon; the Greeks addressed him as Zeus; and the Romans called him Jupiter.

The Jewish historian Lewy says that the divine name of Ham was worshiped as a God by the Semites. G. Buchanan Gray states that the names Am and Ammi are proper names of a God, whereas Dr. William Smith and Professor Horne says the word Am means Ham.29

Mrs. Richardson: Dr. Johnson, when did the color black first exist, and if black represented evil, then why did God create the color?

Dr. Johnson: I would first like to say that God-Eloham and darkness represent infinity, since the two existed before the beginning. Now to answer your question, our earliest acknowledgment of darkness occurred during the very beginning of creation. Before the defiance of Lucifer, the color black or dark was viewed as holy, sacred or divine, since there existed no wrong or sin in the universe! Remember, all was perfect before the rebellion of Lucifer. This information is not difficult to understand by those who study and have the power of the Holy Spirit.30

Mrs. Pinkham: Dr. Johnson, I can think of a lot of evil words in my mind, but you're trying to tell me that before Lucifer sinned, these same words could be viewed as Holy and openly expressed?

Dr. Johnson: Why not? Before the defiance of Lucifer, those same words wouldn't have been contaminated to represent evilness. Remember, Lucifer only redefined those words to represent evil during his war with God-Yahwe, but before that incident there were no evil thoughts or words in the universe!

Mrs. Richardson: Dr. Johnson, why do ministers teach that darkness is evil?

Dr. Johnson: Because their minds lack understanding of the original meaning of darkness which referred to the three catagories of darkness; natural, spiritual, and demonic. The ministers only emphasize the demonic darkness, totally overlooking the natural and divine darkness. Their most critical error (aside from not studying) is defining all darkness with one definition.

Mrs. Richardson: Give me some examples from the Bible referring to the three kinds of darkness.

Dr. Johnson: Well, natural darkness is exemplified in Genesis 1:2; divine in Genesis 15:12–13, I Kings 8:10–12, Zechariah 6:1–6; and demonic, (which only occurs when there exists a mental inadequacy) in I John 2:9–11 and Hosea 4:6.

Mrs. Richardson: Dr. Johnson, explain I John 1:5 that says God is light, and in Him there is no darkness at all.

Dr. Johnson: That particular passage merely reflects on God's ingenious thinking or, may I say, His mental psychic. It merely indicates that in Him there is no unknowing. Some ministers have tragically misinterpreted this verse as indicating a natural or physical darkness.31

Mrs. Pinkham: What do you base your comments on when you say that God and darkness existed before anything?

Dr. Johnson: Well, our first account of God-Hama-Kom is when He thrust Himself out of thick darkness, saying, "Let there be light." Now the chief question to ask is what was around God-Hama-Kom before He said, "Let there be light?" This verse clearly reveals that the world and all power derived out of darkness.32

Mrs. Richardson: So you believe darkness is a phenomenon having an unexplainable character?

Dr. Johnson: Yes, it is just as mysterious as God Himself, since both are holy and primordial. God-Yahwe and darkness are identified as Mysteries or Enigmas; the ancient Greeks called the term enigma, "darkly." According to the Jewish historian Goldziher, the Hebrews worshiped the black sky, since God-Yahwe would so often visit them in the thick black smoke, clouds, and thunderstorms. The Bible also shows the color black as the representation of God-Yahwe as He visited Abraham, Moses, and others in the form of impenetrable darkness. The Hebrews called God-Yahwe, "A Horror of Darkness."33

Pastor Edwards: So you're saying God had an attraction toward darkness?

Dr. Johnson: Sure He did. He concealed Himself and the world's greatest treasures in darkness. He appeared to show an obsession with darkness, like a female's obsession with furs and gems, by joyfully wrapping Himself in darkness. Remember, His pavillion rests in the dark waters and thick clouds of the skies. He journeyed the dark universe and spoke from the black clouds, and visited the ancient laymen, priests, prophets, kings, queens, temples, and tabernacles in the form of awesome darkness.34

Brother Tidwell: So you think darkness is good because God used darkness as a representation of Himself?

Dr. Johnson: Absolutely. Now listen; would God-Jehova use a sinful matter or material to represent Himself? Let's exercise some discretion here. Why is the color black, which is the same as dark, called the glory of God-Jehova in I Kings 8:10–12? If darkness represented inferiority, then why would God-Jehova have such an admiration for it, by wrapping Himself in darkness? If Darkness is evil, then why would God-Jehova use it as a representation of Himself? In ancient times natural darkness was considered as a positive, whereas white represented negative since white was not the original color of the universe. White also represented evil awareness, or knowledge, such as what Adam, or Adham, experienced in the Garden of Eden. Remember, Lucifer means "Bright Light."35

Mrs. Pinkham: Dr. Johnson, give me one good reason of why I should believe darkness is great?

Dr. Johnson: Because you were developed in darkness. You came out of darkness, and you were in your mother's womb for 9 months, which was pitch black dark. Yahwe, the "Greatest of Greatest," first revealed Himself to man coming out of the thick black darkness, saying, "Let there be light!" God-Yahwe says, in Isaiah 45:3, that He will give us the treasures of darkness, and hidden riches of secret places, that we may know that He is God-Yahwe. Remember, Jesus Ham-Ashiah, or Messiah, was born at night, crucified during day, and resurrected in the darkness. Jesus says, "What I say to you in darkness, go ye and say in the light," indicating that the Word, or knowledge comes out of darkness! As previously stated, the Hebrews in Genesis 15: 12-13 called God-Yahwe, "A Horror of Darkness." This information is not difficult to understand by those who study and have the power of the Holy Spirit.36

Mr. Gibbes: Dr. Johnson, if there are three categories of darkness, then what about light?

Dr. Johnson: There are also three categories of light; natural, spiritual, and demonic. The ministers only emphasize the divine and natural light, totally overlooking the demonic light. To define all light with one definition is another critical error of ministers.

Brother Hightower: Dr. Johnson, give us some examples in the Bible concerning the three kinds of light.

Dr. Johnson: Well, natural light is exemplified in Genesis 1:1–3, 30:35, 37; Leviticus 13:3; divine in Revelation 22:16, and demonic in Exodus 4:6–7, II Kings 5:27, Isaiah 14:12, Luke 10:18, and II Corinthians 11:14. Remember, Lucifer or Satan means "Bright Light," and it was he through deception that he created mental confusion. In ancient times natural darkness was considered a positive, whereas white represented negative, since white was not the original color in the beginning. White represented evil awareness, or knowledge, such as what Adam, or Adham, experienced in the Garden of Eden.37

Mrs. Richardson: What you're saying is that there is a lot of biblical truth and beauty involving the term "black" or "darkness."

Dr. Johnson: More than what we will ever comprehend. Not only is black the first color mentioned in the Bible, it is also the only color called "beautiful," which should compel modern scholars to redefine the term black as an alternative word that can represent both negative and positive; life and death; first and last; up and down; left and right; forward and backward; hot and cold; black and white; good and evil; love and hate; beginning and end; before and after, or immortality.38

Mrs. Lott: Dr. Johnson, how can the term Ham, which means black, also represent immortality?

Dr. Johnson: The term "Im" of immortal or immortality is equal to the word "Am," the same as Ham. It was an ancient custom to spell Ham, "Am" or "Im."39

Mrs. Pinkham: Dr. Johnson, isn't that impossible for black to equal the two extremes?

Dr. Johnson: What's impossible about it? We must acknowledge that a single word can represent both negative and positive. For example, the term angel can represent Satan and Gabriel, or good or evil; the term god can define Jehova and Lucifer, or a false or true god; the ancient Greek word "no," meant "yes" in Hebrew. The letter "y" can represent a vowel and consonant; the word "criminalist" can represent a person who commits a crime, as well as one who studies crime.

I could go on and on, but I find it unecessary. Lets refocus on the three catagories of darkness and light, realizing that if there exists a divine light as well as a divine darkness, then the two are characteristically the same, which holds true for an evil light and an evil darkness!

Psalm 139:12 says, "Yea, the darkness hideth not from thee; but the night shineth as the day; the darkness and the light are both alike to thee." The major drawback toward understanding how the essence of black can represent both good and evil, is largely centered around our own mental inadequacy to decipher, unravel, or decode words. The word "black," which is the same as Ham, Cham, Yam, I Am, Elohim, Eloham, Jehova, Yahwe, etc., is equivalent to first and last; white and niger; alpha and omega; death and life; mortal and immortal; and all other extremes. Jesus' comment as being the first and last and the alpha and omega, clearly represent the two extremes. In Revelation 1:18, didn't Jesus say that He was once dead but now alive? Doesn't Isaiah 53:2 speak of our beautiful Jesus as being physically ugly? Another demonstration of God placing His greatest glory and power in dark urly vessels. Biblically, this information is also found in I Corinthians 12:22-24.

Mr. Gibbes: Dr. Johnson, in reference to your last comment concerning Jesus representing the two extremes, well, I believe Jesus to be the first and last, but what does that have to do with Ham?

Dr. Johnson: Let me reiterate that the name Jesus means Ham, Amen, or I Am. Some 2000 years before Jesus, the Ethiopians, Egyptians, and others called Ham, "Amen" and "Hamen," since the word "Am" of Amen was also spelled Ham. In ancient times, the word "Am" automatically inherited the letters "H," "K," "C," "I" and "Y", which changed Am to Hamen, Ham, Kam, Cam, I Am, and Yam. Again, my point is to alert the audience to the fact that Jesus' name, which covers the two extremes, also means Ham or Amen. To be more explicit, the name Messiah, which means Jesus, is a direct translation of the Hebrew word "Ham-Ashiah."40

In Matthew 27:37, and Revelation 17:14, Jesus is called "King of the Jews," and "King of Kings." Saints. Doesn't the biblical term Ham-Melech mean king?

Mrs. Richardson: Dr. Johnson, as a high school English teacher, I'm aware of your earlier description of Ham meaning Cham or I Am since the letter "H" is equivalent to "K" and the "K" to "C" and the "C" to "I," which definitely alters Ham to I Am, or any other name referring to the Supreme Creator.

Lets face it, since the name Ham means Black or Niger, and can be altered to I Am, that should eliminate all doubt concerning Ham in representing the two extremes. I'm convinced that your explanation of Ham in reference to I Am, is one of the world's best kept secrets. This once-concealed but revealing information should influence our churches to alter the Western way of teaching religion and the Bible. But often the truth is a hard pill to swallow. I think it's a disgrace that no other people on earth will so harshly attack their own scholar's account of a biblical heritage as our people. Nevertheless, it shouldn't be ignored that some of our people are conditioned to only accept Black history through the eyes of non-Blacks.

Dr. Johnson: I appreciate your support Mrs. Richardson, but keep in mind of why I was invited here. By all means let the audience be relentless in their questions since there's much to learn.

Mrs. Jefferson: Dr. Johnson, you commented that the name Ham was also known as Cham and Yam, which are translated "I Am." My question is; what ancient nations called Ham, "Yam," and, again, how did the spelling Yam become I Am?

Dr. Johnson: The Arabians and Persians called Ham, "Yam." The letter "Y" of Yam is equivalent to "I," thereby altering Yam to I Am.41

Mr. Jones: Dr. Johnson, the ancient Greeks often defined Nekros or Nekus, which is the same as Negro, as "death." Is that correct?

Dr. Johnson: Yes, but what the Greeks failed to mention (or, may

I say, what modern scholars fail to reveal) is that the same name in Hebrew means "life" or "immortal," and many other definitions. Jesus, whose name is equivalent to I Am, Amen, or Hamen, the same as Ham, also represents death, life or immortal. That's because the term "Im" of immortal is equal to the word "Am," the same as Ham. It was an ancient custom to spell Ham, "Am" or "Im."42

Mr. Jackson: Dr. Johnson, can you furnish more evidence to support your claim that the word "black" or "Ham" covers the two extremes?

Dr. Johnson: Well, I don't have to remind you of how we've been tricked concerning the word "black." But let us not overlook that in Song of Solomon 1:5, this same word is described as beautiful. How strange that the word "black," which has received so much negative attention, is the only color in the Bible called beautiful.

Mr. Jackson: In my Bible it says "comely."

Dr. Johnson: During the translation of the King James Version, the word beautiful, was cunningly replaced by "comely." *The Old Greek Septuagint Version* which was published in 250 B.C., says "black and beautiful."43

Mrs. Richardson: Dr. Johnson the verse is quoted, "I am black, but comely, O ye daughters of Jerusalem, as the tents of Kedar, as the curtains of Solomon." Now my concern is over how the word "but" got in that verse.

Dr. Johnson: Simple. In ancient times the word "but" was interchangeable with "and!"44

Ms. Louis: Dr. Johnson, what difference does it make what color Jesus is?

Dr. Johnson: I would first like to say that I think this question should be addressed to Daniel and St. John who spoke of Jesus' woolly hair and dark skin. In all respect, Jesus' color never makes a difference when it comes to accepting Him as our personal Savior. However, it does makes a difference in respect to honoring the truth; the truth which is the fabric of our lives; the truth by which we live; the truth which preserves the natural order of things.

Let me also stress that Jesus' color is never the prime issue. The topic here is to honor the truth and not bury that truth if it relates to color; an act we're highly guilty of! Ms. Louis, if we believe the Bible to be the holy word of God written by inspired men, then why should we devalue the Scripture that mentions Jesus' skin to be dark, and His hair like pure wool, by saying, "what difference does it make?" Saints, if Jesus' color doesn't make a difference, then why does it upset us when the subject is brought up?45

Mrs. Jackson: Dr. Johnson, you put a lot of emphasis on Jesus' kinky hair and dark skin. Can kinky hair and dark skin save us?

Dr. Johnson: No, but to lie about Jesus Ham-Ashiah, or Messiah's, woolly hair and dark skin can send you to damnation. Remember, the Scripture says that no liars will enter the kingdom of heaven. To lie about Jesus' personal features is also in violation to the ninth Commandment, "Thou shall not bear false witness." The Apostle John Cautioned us not to deny Jesus' flesh. It is no secret that Jesus' skin was blackest-dark.46
Mrs. Pinkham: Dr. Johnson, are you trying to make everybody in the Bible Black?

Dr. Johnson: Absolutely not. I'm only trying to reveal the history of Blacks in the Bible.

Reverend Pierce: Dr. Johnson, I have preached for 50 years, and when I read the Bible I can't see color!

Dr. Johnson: Reverend Pierce, with all due respect, if you actually believe just what you've said, then you probably should stop preaching. Sir, the mentioning of color is first noticed in Genesis 1:1–3, and continues to be voiced throughout the Scriptures. Let me remind you of several passages. Remember in Exodus 4:6–7 and Numbers 12:10 when God-Eloham changed the flesh of Moses and his sister Miriam from dark to white? Have you forgotten that Genesis 25:24–25 speaks of Isaac and Rebekah's twin son Esau being red, while his brother Jacob was of a normal complexion? How can you overlook Job 30:30 that says, "My skin is black upon me," or Jeremiah 13:23 that questions whether an Ethiopian can change his skin? Reverend Pierce, as I have stated, color is exemplified throughout the Bible from Genesis to Revelation. I just can't understand why you and others can't see it!

Mr. Jackson: Dr. Johnson, what is your explanation for why the Bible exists? What is its true purpose?

Dr. Johnson: To promote the truth, the whole truth, and nothing but pure gospel truth!

Bishop Franklin: Dr. Johnson, I marvel at all colors, since all colors were created by God. Colors certainly help us to communicate our ideas and attitudes. Whether we realize it or not, we're governed by color. Daylight and darkness definitely have phenomenal effects on man's behavior, and on all other life. Socially, the NAACP, Affirmative Action, and the Urban League, are about color. The colors of the rainbow are one of man's favorite attractions, and in the *Unger Bible Dictionary* the Hebrews called Yahweh, "Hu." The term "Hu," the same as Hue, is just another expression meaning color.

Dr. Johnson: Bishop Franklin, your expression is well taken.

Reverend Pierce: What does this have to do with salvation?

Dr. Johnson: Salvation, as stated earlier, not only cleanses our souls, but also educates and directs our hearts and minds toward other avenues of learning. Nevertheless, our chosen topic of today isn't centered around redemption, but primarily around how God-Eloham, or Elohim, used Black people in the Bible. Sir, If I'm not mistaken, I wasn't invited here to give this audience a preaching sermon, but a teaching one. Let us remember Solomon's comments in Ecclesiastes 3:1 that says, "There is a season and time to every purpose under the heaven;" and Paul's in I Corinthians 14:40, "let all things be done descently and in order." I'm praying that we will heed to their comments during this section.

Mr. Gibbes: Dr. Johnson are there any other biblical facts to support Jesus' Negroid characteristics?

Dr. Johnson: Jesus' life being threatened by Herod forcing His parents to smuggle Him to Egypt, is evidence of Jesus possessing Negro features. The major question to ask is; why would a white-skinned person hide in an all black nation like Egypt? Remember, the Egyptians during that period were coal black. Now let us not overlook that Jesus' lineage can be traced to the African race, a fact proven throughout the Bible and in natural history.47

Mr. Gibbes: You covered the biblical point, now can you detail some historical facts?

Dr. Johnson: Well, the antiquarians such as Celsus, Plutarch, Tacitus, Eusebius, and Diodorus, all agreed that the original Hebrews were Ethiopians and Egyptians who were forced out of Egypt. In reality, Jesus Christ was a descendant of those people.

Again, I must remind you of Fishberg's comments that indicate that the ancient Hebrews possessed largely Negro features such as woolly hair, dark skin, thick lips that folded, large heads, and projecting jaws.48

Mrs. Pinkham: So you believe that Jesus Christ came out of Africa?

Dr. Johnson: Sure He did. Doesn't Psalm 68: 31; Hosea 11:1; and Matthew 2:14–15 verify this fact? Jesus' ancestry came out of Africa.

Mr. Todd: Don't you think it's wrong to promote Jesus' natural appearance? Have we forgotten that it is the spiritual that will save us, and not the natural?

Dr. Johnson: I'm only obeying the will of God by promoting His wishes. The Scriptures says that every spirit that denies Jesus' natural flesh is not of God, but of the antichrist. This particular verse clearly informs us that a person cannot enter the kingdom of God unless first recognizing Jesus' flesh. Now regarding your second question, I'll only pray that you'll understand that the natural was before the spirit, and that there is a divine nature.49

Mr. Todd: I just can't accept your explanation. I find it hard to believe you.

Dr. Johnson: Mr. Todd it's none of my business whether you believe me or not! My duty is to only obey God's will by spreading His word. It would be to your best interest to read Ezekiel 3:1–5; 18–20; 33:1–9, because your doubts rest in the hands of God not in mine.

Mrs. Jackson: Dr. Johnson, wasn't Jesus an olive-colored person?

Dr. Johnson: Sure he was. However, keep in mind that an olive can be described as a green undeveloped or unripe fetus in the mother's womb, whereas, outside the embryo, the olive, while growing from infant to an adult, changes from a immature yellow, to a matured dark purple, then black. Yes, Jesus was often referred to as olive-looking. The Prophet Ezekiel witnessed Him as Amber or Hamber, which have the colors of brown-black or resin. Jesus Christ, according to Daniel and St. John, fits the resin appearance.50

Sister Payne: Can you name a few of Jesus' Black biblical ancestors?

Dr. Johnson: Yes. Jesus Christ's great-great grandmother was the Negress Rahab, "the Canaanitish." Rahab married a Jew named Salmon, who fathered Boaz; Boaz begot Obed, Obed begot Jesse; Jesse begot David and David fathered Solomon, from whom the Messiah descended. Let us also acknowledge that the name Salmon is equivalent to Zalmon and Solomon, meaning, "dark-skinned man." Solomon was also spelled Salomon; "Sal" of Salomon means "dark colored."51

Sister Payne: But since Jesus was born of a virgin, how could He be a direct offshoot of Solomon going back to Rahab?

Dr. Johnson: Oh, you see, Mary the mother of Jesus Ham-Ashiah, or Messiah, was the daughter of Heli, who was a direct descendant of the Solomonic line, which stretched back to David, Jesse, Obed, Boaz, and Rahab the Negress. I would like to also emphasize that one of Jesus Ham-Ashiah's ancestors was called "Neri," meaning Niger or Black.52

Sister Payne: Dr. Johnson, what source of information will verify that Neri means Niger or Nigger?

Dr. Johnson: This information can be found in Luke 3:27; The Jewish Family Names, by Guggenheimer, p. 546. 1992, and *Webster's Third New International Dictionary.*

Mrs. Pinkham: Dr. Johnson, can knowledge alone save us?

Dr. Johnson: No, since the Bible informs us that knowledge without love profits a man nothing. Yet it informs us that knowledge is one of God-Yahwe's many gifts. Isaiah says that wisdom and knowledge shall be the stability of our time and strength of salvation, whereas knowledge is most important as one of God-Yahwe's riches! Hosea says that his people were destroyed because of a lack of knowledge.53

Mr. Todd: So what? So big deal. After we have listened to your comments, where do we go from here?

Dr. Johnson: It's up to you and the Holy Spirit how you'll apply this information; hopefully by acknowledging that our future depends upon our knowledge of the past, that our past is the pipeline to our future.

Mrs. Pinkham: Dr. Johnson I share some of Mr. Todd's feeling by strongly sensing that you're misleading us!

Dr. Johnson: Mrs. Pinkham, I'm not the institution that reared or nursed you on fairytale lines. I've never taught you and your siblings that George Washington cut down a cherry tree, telling his father that he would never tell a lie, or that a white lie is permissible. I never taught you that you were doomed to failure because you were not credited in God's image, nor that Columbus discovered North America when he didn't. I never told you to despise your features and Mother Africa, so how is it that I'm misleading you?

Mrs. Pinkham: I still feel that you're promoting the color issue.

Dr. Johnson: I'm promoting the truth which just happens to involve the color issue. The Holy Spirit will never conceal the truth based on color.

Mr. Gibbes: Can you name other Blacks who were members of Jesus' genealogy?

Dr. Johnson: Oh sure. The Negress Jezebel, through her daughter Athaliah, spread Negro blood throughout the United Kingdom of Judah, from Joash to Judah's last king, Zedekiah. Zedekiah was an ancestor of Jesus Christ's earthly father Joseph. Now, keep in mind that Mary's father Heli was a descendant of David, who was an ancestor of the Black Judean King Ahaziah, the son of Jehoram and the Negress Athaliah.54

Mr. Coolidge: Dr. Johnson from your own assessment, expound a little more on why Black ministers fail to teach this subject. What is their reaction to your introduction?

Dr. Johnson: There are several reasons why Black ministers fail to teach this subject and one can be attributed to fear. But again, let me stress that all ministers are not blind to this truth, and have promoted the subject as a Bible fact. These ministers realize that all truth is not sweet to hear, that our Bible speaks of a bitter truth as well as a sweet truth, indicating that bitter truth cuts like a two-edged sword. These ministers understand that God does not give the spirit of fear, but gives power, love, and a sound mind. Now in respect to your second question; most ministers will duck this issue by saying, "what difference does it make?" or "it's not important!" This is actually saying that there are Scriptures in the Bible that shouldn't be discussed.55

Ms. Louis: So you feel our souls need bitter and sweet truth?

Dr. Johnson: Sure. By not merging these two truths, we are deprived of having the whole truth!

Mr. Coolidge: Why do you feel ministers make these comments?

Dr. Johnson: Chiefly based upon the fact that the subject involves Black people. Many Black ministers are willing to bury biblical information if associated to color! They seem to contradict themselves by commenting that every verse in the Bible is pure, and then evading most verses relating to black issues. A minister may preach that all things are possible, but when it comes to promoting a non-Jewish and non-White heritage, he immediately takes a cowardly stand as if all things are not possible. He often preaches that John 16:13 says, "let the spirit guide us in all truth," but will deny the very truth the Bible offers him concerning his own heritage. He has a negative answer to nearly every Scripture that reflects his heritage. He constantly reminds us that his prime mission is to promote salvation through the Holy Spirit, but critically fails to inform his congregation that all knowledge of God comes through the power of the Holy Spirit, which doesn't conceal truth based upon color.

The Holy Spirit is not limited and has a function greater than just cleansing the soul. It also has the power to educate individuals toward other avenues of learning; ever revealing the truth, rather then concealing the truth. A minister may even teach that God has no respect of persons, but will himself practice what he claims God forbids by denying his own people their biblical heritage.

The Bible plainly tells the minister that Jesus' hair was like sheep wool, and His arms and feet the color of brass, as if burned in a furnace, yet the Black ministers will continue to preach just the opposite, along with placing a Caucasian picture, with horse mane hair and white skin over their pulpits. How absurd! He will tell his congregation that color makes no difference, but will worship that false Euro-icon until the day he dies. His misled congregation, if ever asked to replace that Euro-picture, with the very description revealed in Daniel 7:9 and 10:6 and Revelation 1:14–15 and 4:3, will fight you with tooth and nail until doomsday! Jesus Christ Himself could appear in our churches tomorrow and would have the fight of His life trying to compel our people to remove those false Euro-images.

Black peoples' desire to praise a White Jesus within their churches, is merely another form of deception. Before the raise of the *Renaissance,* Jesus Christ, and most saints, were depicted in Africa, Asia, and Europe as Blacks. These present day Caucasian-icons of Jesus within our assemblies, have definitely hindered our divine potentials, by preventing positive mental growth. Black peoples' obsession to worship a White Jesus has without a doubt inhibited them from becoming a workable force within a functionable society.

Black ministers who endorse this practice, probably do so because they are a product of *Jim-crow*, or they don't know any better. How sad!

Mr. Coolidge: Dr. Johnson, why do you think Blacks prefer to see Jesus as White?

Dr. Johnson: Because Blacks have been trained and not educated. When a person reads the Bible and can see every race in the Bible, other than his own, then he has been trained and not educated. However, when a person reads the Bible and can observe his race as well as others, then he has been educated. There is a difference! Until we learn this difference, we will remain hundreds of years behind.

Mr. Coolidge, all races are re-examining the Bible and themselves, except Black people, who are still living in self denial. I can clearly understand why the Caucasian, Jewish, and Italian clergies don't take many of our Black ministers seriously, knowing that their own biblical heritage exists right under their noses, without their awareness.

Mrs. Richardson: The blind leading the blind.

Dr. Johnson: You couldn't have described it any better.

Mrs. Richardson: Dr. Johnson, if some of our ministers would apply themselves to II Timothy 2:15 that says, "Study to show thyself approved unto God," that would definitely makes things better.

Dr. Johnson: I agree. Remember Hosea 4:6; "My people are destroyed because of a lack of knowledge."

Bishop Franklin: I would like to comment that Isaiah 28:10 says, "For precept must be upon precept, precept upon precept; line upon line, line upon line, here a little, and there a little." Oh yes saints, we must study.

Ms. Dupree: Dr. Johnson, why do you hold ministers accountable to how we interpret the Scriptures?

Dr. Johnson: Because they are preceived by our society as the defenders of truth and the pillars of the Black community. During and after slavery they played a key role in the advancement of the oppressed. Their performance can determine whether we advance or stagnate by the authority we have entrusted in them.

Not only do I believe we should demand more of our ministers in revealing Spiritual secrets of the Bible, but also in teaching our natural history. Let's face the fact that a minister is only as strong as the people he serves. After all, in a democratic system, isn't there a phrase called "we the people?" Now to address your question directly, if a leader doesn't raise certain issues, then the people will not be stimulated by them. If the Holy Spirit is rooted in our soul, as we often confess, then we shouldn't be afraid to demand advancing knowledge, or to question our minister's ability to decipher the Scriptures, as demonstrated in Acts 17:10–11. We should not just allow them feed us half of the truth.

Doesn't Mark 13:22 say that false Christs and prophets shall rise and, if possible, will deceive the very elect? This is not difficult to understand by those who study and have the power of the Holy Spirit. What are we afraid of? We're only subject to God-Yahwe-Eloham. We must demand that our ministers stop explaining our heritage away based on color!

Ms. Dupree: So you feel most of our ministers are not explaining our biblical heritage because of the church's lack of demand? Why do you feel some congregations lack this demand?

Dr. Johnson: Because of centuries of indoctrination to deny who we are. Most ministers who attend Caucasian theology schools are indoctrinated to transform their own African-views to a Euro-perspective. For example, it is a biblical and historical fact that the name Ham means black in Hebrew, and that he had four Negro African sons named Cush (the same as Ethiopia), Mizraim (translated as Egypt), Phut (interpretated as Libya), and Canaan (meaning Phoenicia, Palestine, Humble, or Hamble). These Negro sons of Ham are chronologically traced throughout the Bible beginning with Genesis 5:32. The ancient terms Ethiopia, Egypt, Libya, and Canaan, were historically, as well as genetically, defined Black.

But the Black ministers after obtaining their Doctorates in an all-white seminary, seem to perceive the opposite, and will button their lip when asked to voice an opinion. They'll confess to have the Holy Spirit which reveals all truth, but will whole-heartedly ignore a biblical passage if it involves their own heritage! When confronted with this behavior, they'll dodge the issue by saying it's not important. Yet, at the same time, they'll loudly promote the Greek and Jewish heritage. What a contradiction! Let me reiterate that all ministers do not fit this description, but definitely more than what we need considering the position they hold.56

Mr. Gibbes: Dr. Johnson, aren't you sort of putting your neck on the line by making such comments?

Dr. Johnson: Any time you oppose Lucifer you're jeopardizing your safety, but let us remember Luke 12:4–5 that says, "Be not afraid of him who can kill the body, but only fear Him who has the power to kill and cast you into hell." Let's face it, we have bad ministers just as we have bad policemen, doctors, and politicians.

Ms. Louis: Dr. Johnson, how would you answer the question if you were asked how you know Blacks are in the Bible?

Dr. Johnson: I would answer by saying to read Acts 17:26, in which it says by one blood were all nations formed. Ms. Louis, if there are over 52 African nations, then where do you think these nations derived? To deny a Black biblical presence would contradict Acts 17:26.

Ms. Dupree: Dr. Johnson, how did you go about tracing Blacks in the Bible?

Dr. Johnson: I used the same methodology that the Jews and Caucasians have used for centuries; by focusing upon Noah's three sons Ham, Shem, and Japheth. Ham, before the flood, was called Black, meaning Negro, Africa, etc. Shem, after the flood, was called Semitic or Hebrew, and Japheth, White or Caucasian.57

Ms. Dupree: How do you know that Ham was Black?

Dr. Johnson: Because the name Ham means Black, according to the ancient African, Hebrew, Greek, and Roman writers.58

Brother Hightower: Dr. Johnson, what impact did Africa have on the Bible?

Dr. Johnson: Africa had a tremendous impact on the early writings of the Bible. For instance, the first nations mentioned in the Bible are African nations; Havilah and Ethiopia. The prophet Moses, who wrote the first five books of the Bible, was born in Africa. The continent of Africa was the mother of the early development of the Bible, from the events to the stories to the writers of the stories.

Brother Tidwell: Dr. Johnson, I believe salvation is the primary issue.

Dr. Johnson: I agree. Salvation means to save, and it would be a lot easier to save people if we only told them the whole truth. That's the botton line.

Mr. Jackson: Dr. Johnson, where did you obtain your source of information to write your book called "The Black Biblical Heritage?"

Dr. Johnson: In the last 25 years, I've traveled throughout Europe and through portions of Asia and Africa studying various ancient sources, and conveying with scholarly-minded citizens.

However, to be candid, my chief source of information was derived from none other than the Bible itself. Blacks are in the Bible, they're just not identified.

Mr. Todd: Dr. Johnson, do you believe everything you read?

Dr. Johnson: No, but every person should believe some of the things they read.

Ms. Dupree: Dr. Johnson, why haven't Blacks been recognized or exposed in the Bible by Caucasian ministers?

Dr. Johnson: Blacks have received some recognition by White ministers, but only behind closed doors. Rarely will we find a White minister exposing a Black biblical presence over the media. There have been a few who have voiced a word or two, but were threatened. In most Caucasian churches, the teaching of a Black biblical presence is just not accepted in their church dialogue.

Ms. Dupree: And why not?

Dr. Johnson: Because it is a topic viewed as unpopular in the Western Hemisphere; chiefly because such subjects will undermine Caucasian Western arrogance or ethnocentrism. Let's face it, Europe's activity in the Bible only covers a span of some 99 years in the New Testament, whereas the Negro participation existed over 4000, plus 99 years, from Genesis to Revelation.

Mrs. Pinkham: Dr. Johnson, how do you know what you're saying is true?

Dr. Johnson: Because I obtained my information from authoritative sources, such as the Bible that speaks about the Negro family of nations.

Mr. Todd: Dr. Johnson how can your book or this subject help race relations?

Dr. Johnson: I feel that the outcome of race relations depends on how we handle the truth. Do we conceal or reveal the truth, realizing that truth never kills but heals. The truth never disassimilates but integrates!

Mr. Coolidge: Dr. Johnson, what methods can we apply to improve family unity?

Dr. Johnson: We should observe the Black families in the Bible and the Spiritual example they left for us. Yet, that's quite difficult if we continue to deny their presence in the Scriptures!

Sister Ford: Dr. Johnson, how do you handle a person who refutes this information?

Dr. Johnson: My assignment is to never push information down one's throat, but to only present the truth. You see, Sister Ford, there's an old saying that follows, "you can lead a horse to water, but you can't make him drink." Jesus says, if a person refuses to hear you, then shake the dust off your feet and move on. Paul elaborates by saying that if a man be ignorant, let him be, meaning that if he doesn't want to pay attention to you, pay no attention to him, because he will continue to be ignorant. So once I've fulfilled my calling with God the outcome rests in the hands of that person. Read Ezekiel 3:1–8, 18–19; 33: 1–9.59

Mr. Gibbes: Dr. Johnson, what must we concentrate on to become more aware of this truth? Give us some specifics in the Bible that will encourage us to have a greater understanding.

Dr. Johnson: Scriptually, we should concentrate on Matthew 6:33 and II Timothy 2:15. Naturally, there are other essential verses.

Sister Payne: Dr. Johnson, how can your book *The Black Biblical Heritage* solve Black people's problems?

Dr. Johnson: *The Black Biblical Heritage* is like a piece of a puzzle by which to help us understand who we are. Remember Hosea 4:6?

Reverend Pierce: Dr. Johnson, aren't you being prejudiced by not mentioning other cultures in the Bible?

Dr. Johnson: Sir, you and other ministers have taught us nothing but cultures of other biblical people. For many generations all we've heard was the history of Jews, Greeks, and Italians. It appears that you and your peers have totally disregarded our physical presence in the Bible. Reverend Pierce, had you and your colleagues expounded earlier on the Negro presence in the Bible, you probably would have discovered where the European culture derived, since civilization originated outside of Europe. It is scripturally true that God-Jehova shows no respect of persons, but it is a surety that our ministers have, by ignoring and covering up the Black biblical presence.60

Mr. Jackson: Dr. Johnson, why should we believe you rather than the Caucasian version?

Dr. Johnson: Well, based on what I have researched, the Caucasian version is one-sided, whereas *The Black Biblical Heritage* represents all of God's creations!

Sister Ford: You mentioned the Queen of Sheba in your introduction. Dr. Johnson, what verses and historical facts indicate that she was Black?

Dr. Johnson: Jesus Christ called Sheba, "The Queen of the South." Now isn't Africa South of Israel? The great Jewish historian Flavius Josephus says that Sheba was Queen of Ethiopia and Egypt. Josiah Priest called Sheba a Black woman, who was Ham's posterity.61

Mr. Gibbes: Dr. Johnson, how do you account for the fact that Arabia is also south of Israel?

Dr. Johnson: True, but let us keep in mind that in ancient times Arabia was first called Ethiopia and East Africa. Biblically, the Ethiopians swarmed the entire Arabian peninsula.62

Mrs. Lott: Dr. Johnson, were all three wise men Black? I noticed in your introduction you used the phrase wise "men" and not wise "man."

Dr. Johnson: The three wise men, Melchior the elder, Balthasar the middle-aged, and Gaspar the beardless youth, were, without a doubt, "Blacks" who were led by God-Eloham to visit the Child-Christ. Melchior was from Nubia-Ethiopia; Balthasar, whose name means Black, was also from Ethiopia, whereas Gaspar, the same as Jasper, Caspar, and Kaspar, was from Tyre of Canaan. I would like to also emphasize that the letter "G" of Gaspar is interchangeable with "C" and "K." The term "Gas," "Cas," or "Kas," of Gaspar, was anciently called Cus, Cush, Kus, Kush, meaning Ethiopia, Black, Negro, Niger, or Nigger. The Egyptian term "Per" of Jasper meant house, home, Hame or Ham. Keep in mind that Per is equivalent to Par, since all vowels are equal.63

Bishop Franklin: Dr. Johnson, how can *The Black Biblical Heritage* help our young people?

Dr. Johnson: Well, it could give our youth a wider range in selecting their heroes other than in sports. It will enable them to know that there were many Blacks who walked and talked with the

Father and Son. It's all about education!

Bishop Franklin: Dr. Johnson, how can *The Black Biblical Heritage* help the White and Black friction around the globe?

Dr. Johnson: I pray that The Black Biblical Heritage will help bridge the gap of communication between the two races by enabling us to find a common ground. We must continue to understand that God shows no respect of persons and that there's a beauty in us all that God designed to bring us together.

One of those beauties happens to exist in John 8: 32 in which it is pointed out that one must acknowledge the truth to acquire harmony.

Dr. Carey: Dr. Johnson, what makes your book different from other books about Blacks in the Bible?

Dr. Johnson: Well, according to the *Cokesbury Magazine,* Winston Derek Publishers, and Lushena Books, *The Black Biblical Heritage* is the first book of its kind, other than the Old and New Testaments, to be published in North America and acknowledge a Black presence in the Bible. Unlike most books, *The Black Biblical Heritage* contains study guides.

Brother Hightower: Dr. Johnson, I am convinced that Mary's biblical genealogy is traced to the Solomonic line through her father Heli, which in turn is linked to the Negress Rahab. Now my question is; what modern evidence proves Mary to be Black?

Dr. Johnson: There is much evidence throughout the globe to substaniate Mary being Black. The Polish Pope, John Paul II, and over 36 million White Polish people, continue to honor a Black Mary. This practice is also exercised throughout Spain and other nations. The Virgin Mary was first praised as Black before White.

The new concept of Mary as a Caucasian first came into play during the Renaissance, by Michelangelo, who used his family to pose for the new paintings of Mary, Jesus, and Joseph. It was following this experience that the world began to see the three as Whites.64

Melissa: Dr. Johnson, I'm 12 years of age, and I'm the daughter of Bishop Franklin. What evidence, other than what you've already given, could help me obtain a clearer visual image of how Mary looked?

Dr. Johnson: I hope my response will not appear unnatural to you, but the best course of action is to go home and look at yourself in the mirror!

Melissa: So if my brother asked you a similar question about Jesus, would you give him the same response?

Dr. Johnson: Yes I would, because Jesus had dark skin and wool hair just as your father and brother have.

Melissa: If a White lady looked in the mirror, would she also see an image of Mary?

Dr. Johnson: Of course she would! Melissa, by no means am I trying to discard Whites from being members of the image of God's creation. My principal objective is to introduce enough evidence to you, so you'll no longer exclude your own physical presence in the image of God's creation.

Melissa: How would a White woman favor Mary, if Mary herself wasn't White?

Dr. Johnson: Other then the two being females, there would exist no other similar resemblance since Mary was not White, but a dark-skinned Mediterranean woman. Melissa, any rookie scholar would inform you that the ancient dwellers of the Mediterranean coast, were definitely not white-skinned, but black or dark.

Melissa: But Dr. Johnson, the present dwellers of Israel are not black or dark-skinned.

Dr. Johnson: That's because the present dwellers of Israel are not the original people Moses led out of Egypt. Those dwellers of today's Israel are merely people of European descent who colonized Israel in 1948 through the endorsement of Great Britain and the United States. The average Israeli citizen will tell you that they have no genetic relationship with Abraham, but are only called Jews by obtaining an Israeli citizenship. Doesn't the Scriptures make mention of those of the synagogue confessing to be Jews who are not? The ancient Jews that Moses led out of Egypt were a black-skinned Negroid people.65

Ms. Dupree: Dr. Johnson, comment more on the Apostle Simon the Canaanite. Were the Apostles Black?

Dr. Johnson: The Apostle Simon was called Simon the Canaanite because of his descent from Ham through Canaan. The Hamitic Simon was a Jew by nationality and culture, not through genealogy, since he was a descendant of Ham. The Apostles or Disciples, without a doubt, were Black. Knowing that a great multitude went to arrest Jesus Christ and couldn't recognize Him among His Disciples, is evidence that the Disciples' complexion and hair resembled Jesus' who happened to be Black with woolly hair. This information is not difficult to understand by those who study and have the power of the Holy Spirit.66

Ms. Dupree: Can you substantiate your belief with Scripture?

Dr. Johnson: Well, let's focus on the Apostle Paul. In the book of

Acts, Paul was mistaken as an Egyptian by a chief captain. Now, if Paul was blond with blue eyes and white skin, then why would the chief captain question him concerning his race, knowing that the Egyptians of his day were a black and brown skinned race?67

Reverend Pierce: Dr. Johnson, could you comment on I Timothy 1:4, when Paul advised Timothy to avoid fable and endless genealogies. Do you think it right to teach genealogy?

Dr. Johnson: Let me first acknowledge that God-Eloham encouraged genealogy by reminding the Hebrews to remember Him as the father of Abraham, Isaac, and Jacob, whom the Hebrews were descendants. Jesus Himself reminded the Jews that they were of the seed of Abraham, and that He was a descendant of David. Paul often spoke and boasted of his genealogy from Benjamin. Now the prime question should be; what was Paul's message to Timothy? Reverend Pierce, I think that you and I will agree that we shouldn't promote fables, but remember, Paul never directly said to avoid genealogy, but "endless" genealogy, meaning not to become obsessed with genealogy. Let's face it audience, the Bible is full genealogy.

Remember Jesus' genealogical tree in Matthew 1:1–17 and Luke 3:32-38. If genealogy is wrong then why is it Scripturally promoted? My final comment on this subject is that Blacks in particular have never become obsessed with a Biblical genealogy because of their self denial. It is the Jews and Whites who have constantly violated I Timothy 1:4. The only time I Timothy 1:4 applies to Blacks is when Blacks hint on the subject.68

Sister Payne: Dr. Johnson, what question is most often asked during your presentations?

Dr. Johnson: "What does this have to do with salvation?" and

"What different does it make?" Sad to say, these ridiculous comments are mostly made by Blacks. I am convinced that this bizzare behavior is socially embedded in the collective subconscious. Jews and Whites honorably acknowledge their biblical heritage and will even support a Black heritage, while Blacks remain in denial.

Mrs. Richardson: Where do you think this behavior derived from?

Dr. Johnson: From our teachers who fail to teach the whole Bible which would automatically reveal our true heritage. Yes, it is the fault of our own teachers who seem to know the letter, but lack the zeal of God-Yahwe. This information is not difficult to understand by those who study and have the power of the Holy Spirit!

Brother Tidwell: You mentioned that Simon was called Niger. Why was he called Niger and how should we pronounce the spelling, "Niger?"

Dr. Johnson: Simon, who was a prophet at the church of Antioch, was called Niger because he was an African Black. The term "Niger" is pronounced Nigger and not Ni-jer. Let us be aware that the ancient word "Niger" possessed a different connotation than today's expression. The ancient pronunciation meant all the positives, such as God, King, Supreme, pure, just, honest, beauty, elegant, etc.

There are many ways to understand how the word Niger became a synonym of God. But let us first acknowledge the ancient Ethiopian and Egyptian word for God, which was spelled "Neter," the same as Niger, since the letter "T" of Neter was interchanged with "C," which was developed from the letter "G." The Latin "T" was also written "C" in Old French. The term Ham which means Black and Niger, is a suffix of Israel's God Eloham, the same as Elohim, since the Hebrew letter "A" was interchangeable with "I." The name Ham is also a prefix of the Hebrew word Ham-Ashiah, meaning Messiah, Jesus and King. The term Ham, Hama, Kam, or Kom, also equals the Hebrew term Hama-Kom, meaning God. The Holy word "Ni" of Niger is revealed in the oldest found written Bible, which the Negro Egyptians called "The Egyptian Book of Light." The Egyptians defined the Deity Ni as a watery abyss from which all things evolve. The term "Ni" is merely an ancient synonym of Him, Ham, No, Ne, Amon, Amen, or Amen-Ra, a name which in Revelation 3:14, is addressed to Jesus.

The Babylonians called Ni, "Our God." The historian Rogers says the term "Ni" probably meant "great." But had Rogers observed the word "Om-Ni-Potent," which means "God Almighty," he would have likely omitted the word "probably," since the term "Ni" is observed in the word Om-Ni-Potent. The prophet Daniel associated the word "Ne" of Me-Ne to God. The term Ni, Ne, Na, Nu, No, and Ny were ancient terms meaning "Great God," whereas "Ger" (Gar) of Niger signified God and Water!69

Brother Tidwell: So you prefer that we call the word Ni-jer, "Nigger" or "Niger?"

Dr. Johnson: True, I hope we'll never forget the word's original pronunciation. If you wouldn't pronounce the word Tiger, "Ti-jer," then why pronounce Nigger or Niger, "Ni-jer?"

Bishop Franklin: Dr. Johnson, your explanation is electrifying. Now, how did the term "Nigger" with the extra consonant "g" come into play? I assume the spelling Niger and Nigger are the same?

Dr. Johnson: Yes, the spellings are the same. The word "Nigger" with the double "g" was anciently spelled with a single "g," meaning God, King, Supreme, etc., throughout Africa and Asia. The word "Niger" with one "g," was used as far back as 425 B.C. during the Greek Herodotus' era. The term continued to be spelled with a single "g," up until the time of Noah Webster, who, after researching the word's authenticity, chose to distort the term by adding an extra "g," then internationalizing the word to be derogative.

Ms. Dupree: Dr. Johnson, why did Webster alter the spelling from one "g" to two?

Dr. Johnson: He really had no choice after discovering its true meaning. Remember, Webster's new dictionary emerged on the American scene, when slavery was at an all-time high. For Webster to have defined the ancient term "Niger" to mean God would have definitely caused an American outrage, since the name Niger or Nigger was well known in the Euro-mind to represent inferiority!

Bishop Franklin: Dr. Johnson, I would like you to elaborate more on the Ethiopian word "Negus," meaning King. Does Negus also means Niger?

Dr. Johnson: Yes, the term Negus means Negro, Black, or Niger. The word Negus is also equivalent to the word Nego, and the word Nego means God and Negro.70

Mrs. Richardson: Dr. Johnson, if the word Niger means God, King, and Supreme, than why is the word so resented in modern times?

Dr. Johnson: Well, didn't Jesus say in Matthew 10:22 that, "They shall hate you for my name's sake?" The names I Am and Messiah can be transliterated, "Niger." The word "I Am" is

65

noneother then Ham, since the letter "I" was anciently exchanged for "C," the "C" for "K" and the "K" for "H," thereby altering I Am to Ham. The word Messiah is merely a translation of the Hebrew word Ham-Ashiah. Again, the name Ham means Black, Niger, Negro, I Am, God-Elohim or Eloham, God-Yahwe, God-Jehova, God-El Shaddai, etc.71

Mr. Todd: Dr. Johnson, Am I hearing you right? Are you actually saying the word Nigger or Niger means God?

Dr. Johnson: Let me define the term from a different perspective. When the word Niger is pronounced, it is merely an old ancient expression meaning "Master you are my God, I am here to worship you!"

Mr. Jackson: Based on what evidence?

Dr. Johnson: Based on the fact that the sacred name Ham means Black, Niger, or Negro, which, in turn, means Messiah-Jesus and God. People, when you say "Jesus," you're merely saying Ham or Niger. Doesn't Jesus mean Messiah? Well, the term Messiah is a direct translation of the Hebrew word Ham-Ashiah! Doesn't "Ham" of Ham-Ashiah mean Black, Negro, Niger, or Nigger? This informatiom is not difficult to understand by those who study and have the power of the Holy Spirit.72

Dr. Laney: Dr. Johnson, we believe from a Christian perspective that God and His true name is supreme in power. To hear, speak, or even contemplate "The Supreme Creator's" real name will have a profound effect on one's psyche or existence! My comment is slightly centered around Moses' experience on Mt. Sinai, in Exodus 33:18, 20–23. Now, the true name of "The Supreme Creator," is not God, Jehova, Yahwe, or any other title given by the Jews and Europeans. These are merely substituted terms to avoid using His real name. Fragments of this information can be found in Exodus 6:3, with the exception of the fact that the name Jehova only appeared in Bibles during the 12th Century. Other than that, the name was never publicly applied.

Dr. Johnson: I agree whole heartedly that the words God and Jehova were not the original names of the "Supreme Creator." The name Johova or Jehovah, as you have explained, only occurred in the 12th-Century Latin Bibles as a mere translation of the name Yahwe or Yahweh.

This treacherous maneuver was only conducted to evade the use of the name "Niger." The modern name, God, was originally called Niger; a term that was and still remains forbidden or unfavorable to pronounce, because of its sacredness! In ancient times, if a person other than a priest uttered the sacred word "Niger," he or she was publicly put to death! Therefore, to avoid the use of the sacred word "Niger," the antiquarians substituted the term with Om or Am, meaning Him, Ham or Black, which later became known as Omen, Amen, Hama-Kom, Hamma-Qom, Eloham, Elohim, Hu (Hue), Shem (Sham), Hamme-Phor-Ash, Yahwe, Adonai, Jehova, El Shaddai, Allah, God, etc.73

Mrs. Lott: Dr. Johnson, how did the translators derive the name Jehova?

Dr. Johnson: They applied the method that I've constantly mentioned throughout this section; researching letters that are interchangeable. The 12th-Century Latin word "Jehovah" or "Jehova," is merely a translation of the Egyptian word "Yahwe," which was introduced to the Hebrews by Moses. The Hebrew "Y" is exchanged for the Anglo "J," the "E" for "A" and the "W" for "V." This created the term "Jehova."

Mr. Todd: Dr. Johnson, your claim that the sacred name Yahwe is an African word is one of the most ridiculous comments I've heard from your mouth. How can you prove such nonsense?

Dr. Johnson: Calm yourself, Mr. Todd, because he who throws mud loses ground. Now, to your comment, the term "Yahwe" was used throughout Africa many centuries before Abraham and Moses (who wrote the Hebrew "Torah" or "Hamash") were born. The term "Yahwe" was first introduced to the Hebrews by Moses at the foot of Mt. Sinai; a name he learned while living among the Negro Egyptians who educated him in religion and science! This is a known and recorded fact. See me after this section and I'll supply you with references.74

Dr. Laney: Dr. Johnson, the most hated spoken word in the universe is the word "Nigger." Just the sound alone seems to stagger man's senses. No word in the universe should have that much power but the name of God-Elohim. Now the fact that the word Niger means Black or Ham, and Ham can be translated to I Am by altering the letter "H" to "K;" the "K" to "C" and the "C" to "I," surely proves that God's name means Niger! How is it that scholars and scientists who can reach the moon can't understand this?

Dr. Johnson: They have always known this truth, but they have been compelled to distort the Scriptures, regardless of the warning in Revelation 22:18–19. The second tragedy is that many Black ministers will not research the subject. Instead, they hold on to the old cliche of "what difference does it make?" How absurd!

Dr. Laney: The name "Niger" reminds me of Hebrews 4:12 that says that the word of God will cut an individual sharper than any two-edged sword, piercing and separating the soul, spirit, joints, and marrow; it judges the reflections and thoughts of the heart.

Dr. Johnson: The genuine name of "The Supreme Creator" has a similar if not equal impact. To hear, speak, or even contemplate the true name of God will have a profound effect on a one's psyche. The brain and its mental faculties are immediately electrified upon the very hearing, speaking, and the mere thought of God's original name "Niger." The name "Niger" is the most powerful word in the world; having as much an effect on the human brain as a hydrogen bomb; leaving its victims in a permanent hallucinatory state of trauma, as if an electrical current has passed through the body! There is no other word in man's comprehension that has such a phenomenal impact on his psyche other than "God." Today's beloved terms such as Yahwe, Jehova, and other diminutives don't evoke the same spontaneous stimulant as God's true name "Niger." God's real name "Niger" is resented daily, rejected and hated more than the terms Lucifer or Devil; both of whom God is greater than. Shameful to say, many individuals would rather be called Satan than the name Niger, especially Blacks, who have not yet committed themselves to research the authenticity of the sacred name "Niger."[75]

Mr. Coolidge: Dr. Johnson could you comment on the origin of religion?

Dr. Johnson: I would first like to recite several comments from leading scholars. The Byzantium Stephanus, while commenting on the universal ancient world, spoke of Ethiopia as the first nation on earth. Stephanus went on to say that the Ethiopians were the first people to introduce the worshiping of the Gods and who enacted laws. The Negro Catholic, St. Augustine, says that what we now call the Christian faith, existed among the ancients; from the time of first man to Jesus Christ in the flesh. This true religion which had already existed began to be called Christianity in Acts 11:26.

Mr. Higgins says that the belief of many Christian writers that the Bible is the oldest Sacred book, is merely supposition. Higgins makes this comment because the Bible and its ideas were written before Moses. The Jewish Historian Bernal says that it was only following the collapse of the Egyptian religion in the second century A.D., that other Asian cults and Christianity began to replace it. Weigall says that the Egyptians, on several occasions, prophesied the coming of the Messiah-Savior. One prophesy, dated about 2200 B.C., read: "He shall be the Shepherd of His people, and in Him there shall be no sin; when His flocks are scattered He shall gather them together." Houston says that the expectation of a coming Messiah-Savior was recorded on the Babylonian tablets prior to 2000 B.C. From these ancient accounts, religion, without a doubt, originated on the African Continent.76

Mrs. Lott: Dr. Johnson, if religion originated on the African Continent, then how did Judaism, Christianity, and Mohammedanism come about?

Dr. Johnson: The Judaic religion was grafted out of the ancient African religious system which laid the foundation that brought forth Christianity and Mohammedanism! Remember that Moses, while attending the Egyptian Mystery school, learned of this religion from his Egyptian Negro lecturers; knowledge that was spoken of in the Bible from Genesis to Deuteronomy. This same religion was then passed on by proceeding prophets. The Hebrews worshiped their God in black, a custom they inherited from the Egyptians.77

Mr. Gibbes: Dr. Johnson, are you saying the Bible didn't originate with the Hebrews?

Dr. Johnson: I am, because the world's oldest written religion was discovered in Africa. This religion can be found in the Egyptian Book of the Light, which the British call, *The Egyptian Book of the Dead*. Every idea, aspect, or description of Judaism, Christianity, and the Mohammedan religion can be found in this book.78

Mr. Gibbes: What Bible Scripture indicates that the Africans knew of Jesus before the Hebrews?

Dr. Johnson: One significant indication is found in Psalms 87:1–7. The verses clearly point out that the concept of the Messiah was born in the minds of the Negro family of nations, long before Abraham or Moses were born. The Egyptians, on several occasions before Abraham and Moses, prophesied the coming of the Messiah-Savior.

The ancient world expected Jesus or Amen (Hamen) to spring from the Negro family of nations. The Apostle Peter recognized this prophesy by saying: "Those forms which were merely mythological forms in the past, are now incarnated and actual in our Savior...." Peter was actually saying that what Negro Ethiopia and Egypt believed became reality even though some thought it to be false.79

Bishop Franklin: Dr. Johnson, what other names did the Ethiopians and Egyptians call their sacred books or Bible?

Dr. Johnson: The books of Ham or Osiris. The Hebrews acquired their Bible through Moses. He learned from the Negro Egyptians that they called the Sacred writings Humash, Hamash, Hami-Sha, Torah, Law, or Five; meaning Ham!80

Dr. Laney: How does Law and Five mean Ham?

Dr. Johnson: The Egyptian word Cemis, Kemis, Hemis or Hamis means Law. The Hebrew and Arab word Five means Ham. The Greek word Pentateuch also means Ham, Hamash, Humash, Hami-Sha, Torah, Law, or Five.81

Bishop Franklin: Dr. Johnson, are any books of the Bible named after Ham? If so, how many?

Dr. Johnson: Actually all books of the Bible are named after I Am or Ham, since all sounds and conceivable thoughts are traced to one common origin; "I Am" or "Ham." Everything that exists is God, I Am, or Ham.

Now getting back to your question, in the *Haxaglota Bible,* and many of the Old German Bibles, the first five books of the Bible are called Mose I, II, III, IV, V, meaning Moses. The name Moses in the *Jewish Family Names and Their Origins*, is called Mor, Neger, or Negro, which means Black or Ham. The books of Kings means Ham, since King in Hebrew is pronounced Ham-Melech, Ham-Mashiah, Ham-Massiah, Ham-Elehk, Ham-Melek, or Ham-Ashiah. The Book of Nahum means Ham, since "Na" of Nahum is another ancient term for Ham. "Hum" of Nahum also means Ham, since the vowel "U" of Hum, is exchanged with "A." The book of Amos means Ham, since "Am" of Amos is translated Ham, whereas "Os" means God.[82]

Dr. Carey: Dr. Johnson, are you saying that the ancients called Moses a Niger or Black?

Dr. Johnson: Yes, in reference to ancient and contemporary literature. Let's first examine the Scriptures in Exodus 4:6–7 where God demonstrated His power to Moses, by instructing him to place his hand in his bosom. When Moses did accordingly and then withdrew his hand, the hand suddenly appeared white. When God ordered Moses to repeat the process, the same snowy-white hand returned to its normal color.

Now the chief question to ask is; what color was Moses' hand before it turned white? The Jewish Rabbi Silver says that movie directors, Sunday school instructors, and grandparents, can be forgiven if they view Moses to have been white, but world's scholars should know better since Moses' cultural lineage indicated he was dark! The Reverend Armistead called Moses a

Colored man since he was an Israelite. Moses was often called a Black man throughout the East.83

Reverend Jason: Dr. Johnson you commented that all conceivable thoughts can be traced to one common origin, I Am or Ham. Give us some example to support this belief.

Dr. Johnson: The name "Ham" is used in our everyday activities, especially in today's worshiping. The word Amen (the same as Hamen which is an old form of the Ethiopian and Egyptian's term for Ham or Hamy-Ne) is frequently used to begin and end petitions. The phrase, "Sing that hymn," is the same as "sing that Ham" since the letter "Y" of hymn is equivalent to "A," "E," "I," "O," "U," whereas the ancient "N" was interchangeable with "M." To say, "hum that tune or song," is the same as "Ham that tune or song." The comment "calm yourself, " is the same as "Ham, cam, or came yourself," since "calm" is an old form of "cam" and "came. "

Remember, the Hebrew, Latin, and French way of pronouncing Ham, is Cam and Cham. To say "let's jam," is another way of saying "let's Ham," since the Hebrew "Y" is equal to the Anglo "J;" the *"J"* to *"Y,"* the *"Y"* to *"I,"* the *"I"* to *"C,"* the *"C"* to *"K"* and the *"K"* to *"H."* "God bless America," is the same as "Eloham bless Ham" since *Am-* or *Ame-* of America means Ham. The term Ri, the same as Re or Ra, also means Ham, whereas -Ca or -Ka of America too means Ham or spirit. To say "I love my home" is the same as "I love my Hom, Hame, or Ham." To say "wisdom," is the same as saying "God- Ham," since Ha-Ham means wisdom in Old Hebrew and Ethiopian.

To comment that Jesus is a lamb (sheep), is the same as saying, "Jesus is a Ham or Hamal, since lamb is a transliteration of Hamal or Ham. To remark "Jesus' blood saved me," is the same as Jesus' *Hemo-, Hama-,* or *Ham* saved me," since blood is called

Hemoglobin, and Hamoglobin in Old German. Paul's comment, "By one blood were all nations formed," is the same as saying, "By one Ham or hamoglobin were all nations formed." To say "my people," is the same as saying, "my Hammi, Hami, Ham, Am, Ammi, or Ami." God's comment: "Blessed be Egypt my people, is the same as saying, "Blessed be Black or Ham my people," since the term Black is equivalent to the words Egypt and Ham. To comment that "Jesus was born in Bethlehem," is the same as saying, "Jesus was born in the house of Ham," since *Beth* means house, whereas *Le* and *Hem,* indicate *Ham.* To say *Resurrection,* is the same as saying *Ham,* since the term for resurrection is pronounced *Hammethim.*

The comment, "Jesus gave up the Ghost," is the same as saying, "Jesus gave up the Ham," since *ghost* in Sweden means Hamn or Ham. Jesus' comment, "I Am the Bread of life," is the same as saying, "I Am the Ham of life," since *bread* in Hebrew is pronounced *Hames* or *Ham.* The ancient translation of Ham meant Cham, I Am, Yam, I Ham, All, Self-Existence, Excellent, God, Head, Gorgeous, First, Niger, Creator, Master, Omega, Ng, Ox, Wonderful, Beautiful, Merciful, Love, Happy, Peace, Order, Sweet, Bread, Cake, Water, Meat, Savior, Infinity, Adam (Ad means God; Am means Ham), or God-Ham, etc. The words Him, Bethlehem, and Elohim are equivalent to Ham, Bethleham and Eloham. When the names of Cush or Ethiopia, Mizraim or Egypt, Phut or Libya, and Canaan are spoken, be assured that the terms God, Ham, Black and Africa are synonymous or inseparable in meaning!

Modern scholars, especially the clergy, have cunningly hidden the multiple meanings and spellings of the term Ham. This millennium old exploitation has covered-up much vital universal interest, in relating to the synonymy of God-Eloham, Adam, and Ham, whose names are a contraction of one. Let it be remembered that the ancient world addressed the Supreme Creator as

God-Ham, the same as Eloham. Since the letter "A" of Ham was interchangeable with "I," both meant God. The term Ham in every respect remains the prime facet of man's total conceptualization; an awareness that most individuals fail to understand. This miscomprehension is probably caused by the different spellings and interpretations of Ham, since the name Ham can be spelled Hem, Him, Hom, Hum, Hym, Hymn, Am, Em, Im, Om, Um, Ym, etc., meaning Eloha, Eloham, Elohim, Ra, Amen-Ra, etc.

The term Ham is as lucrative to man's earthly life, as the very air he breathes. However, due to the lack of interest in interpreting and translating words, the name *Ham* is often misconstrued. The ancients called *Eloham,* Life, The Universe, Food, Fire, etc., and *God-Ham* is synonymous with *Elohim.* For example, the ancients' interpretation of the sun, rain, soil, etc., meant *Ham.* Let it be acknowledged that the very groove of our thoughts and essence of our conversation involves God-Ham or Elohim, same as Cham or Yam, which is translated *I Am,* since *"CH"* and *"Y,"* stand for *"I."*

The antiquarians also referred to the Deity Ham as the Sun, Heat, Hot, Sol, Hu, Hue, He, Heli, Helius, Helio, Heliopolis, On, Diopolis, Hellen, Memphis, Thebes, Amon, Ammon-Zeus, Zeus-Hammon, Jupiter-Amen, Baal, Baal-Ham-On, Ham-On, No, Ne, Ni, Nu, Na, Ng, New, Newt, No-Amon, Ham-On-No, Osiris, Ox, Cow, Ram, Lamb, Sheep, Buck, Alpha, Amen-Ra, Yes, Amen, Jesus, Yah, Yaho, Yahwe, Adham, Hama-Kom, Absolute, Nothing, Everything, Omnipotent, Omega, etc.

Reverend Jason: Dr. Johnson, what documentation will indicate that the terms Amen, Ame, blood, bread and resurrection mean Ham?

Dr. Johnson: See me after this section, and I'll supply you with a host of references.84

Tim: Dr. Johnson, I'm 10 years old and I'm the son of Mrs. Richardson. I'm wondering from which of Noah's three sons the Indians descended?

Dr. Johnson: According to ancient records, the Indians of Asia and America are the offspring of Ham through Cush. I can furnish dozens of references regarding this subject following this section.85

Bishop Franklin: Dr. Johnson, when will the world begin understand this information?

Dr. Johnson: As previously mentioned, most people around the globe have already accepted this information with the exception of Black Americans. This miscomprehension by Black Americans is centered around our own inability to develop the self autonomy that can be one of our many avenues to freedom. Self autonomy helps a person to exercise independent thinking, the pursuit of happiness, and the freedom to determine self predestination. This description does not fit Black America. We depend on a system that educates us to be subordinate.

It is commonly known that if a non-White tries to reach the highest pinnacle, new laws are enacted to retain that person as a subordinate. Self autonomy is one of the highest virtues of government and the human spirit. To deprive a people of this natural virtue will certainly create dependency.

Bishop Franklin: How does this description relate to Blacks and the Bible?

Dr. Johnson: Well, believe it or not, Black people are constantly coerced to evade a Black biblical presence, and as long as they continue to support these tactics then one can be assured that we have another 100 years to go!

Bishop Franklin: What will it take to change this attitude?

Dr. Johnson: The Black congregation will have to make a complete surrender to God, and God will teach them the whole truth. They will have to focus more on Matthew 6:33; John 16:13; II Timothy 2:15; I Timothy 4:13, and Isaiah 28: 10, rather than focusing on those who are either blind to the truth, or just don't care about promoting the whole truth! With those Scriptures, we must implement our uniqueness to one accord. If we fail to accomplish this goal, then our future is bleak.

Mr. Gibbes: Dr. Johnson, if all words mean Ham, then expound on the word *heaven.*

Dr. Johnson: Well, the ancient Ethiopian and Hebrew terms for heaven were Cham, Kham, Ham, Hame, Hama, Sam, Sama, Shame, Sham, I Am, I Ham, Shama, Shamayim, Shamya, Samayim, Chamayim, Hamayim, Chemis, Thebes; same as the Hindi Cama, Sama, Ri, and Car meaning Ham. Heaven in Old French and German is called Hemel, Himel, Hemmel, Himmel, or Himil. In Persian, Sam-Az-Ham, means *High Heaven.* The Persian term Hima-Ka and Hama-Ni-As-Mam also mean *above* or *the whole celestial sphere.* In Japan, Heaven is pronounced *Ame* (Hame), Kami or Ham. Heaven in Croatian and Russian means Nebo, whereas Nebo means Nego or Negro. The Greek term "Kama-Ra" is believed to be a correlation of heaven. In recent times, heaven was addressed *Niger Heaven.* Ham in Old English meant Kingdom of Heaven or a heavenly dwelling place! In Sweden, heaven is pronounced Ham-Na, and in Iceland, Him-Ni. In ancient China, lower heaven was called Kama, the same as Hama or Ham. In Old Germany, Himmelreich means *Heavenly*

Kingdom. The ancient Greeks called heaven, *Olympia*, which was Ham.86

Mr. Jones: Dr. Johnson, I've noticed throughout this section that you've used the term Niger quite frequently. That word troubles most Blacks, so why do you continue to use it?

Dr. Johnson: Why not? When you say God and Jesus, you're saying Niger. Didn't the Hebrews call God *Elohim* and *Hama-Kom*? The term *Elohim* is none other than God-Ham or God-Nigger or Niger, since *Elo* of Elohim is the same as Eli meaning God. The ancient letters *"O"* and *"I"* were interchangeable, whereas -Him of Elohim means Ham, since the ancient "I" and "A" were also interchangeable. The term *Hama-Kom* is none other than *Niger-Niger* or *Nigger-Nigger*, since Hama- of Hama-Kom is the same as Ham meaning Black, Negro, Niger, or Nigger. *Kom* of Hama-Kom is the same as Hom or Ham, since the ancient letter *"K"* was exchanged for *"H,"* and *"O"* for *"A."*

Isn't Jesus called the Messiah and isn't the Greek term Messiah a direct translation of the Hebrew word Ham-Ashiah?" Throughout the centuries Jesus was called Jeshuah Ham-Mashiah and Jescua Ham-Massiah, meaning Jesus Messiah. Dosen't the word Ham mean Black, Negro, Nigger, or Niger? As stated earlier, Blacks fail to understand this fact because of two major factors; they are incapable of exercising independent thinking in relating to a biblical heritage, along with being unable to interpret and translate words. Let me conclude with Hosea 4:6; "My people are destroyed because of a lack of knowledge." Black people totally ignore Matthew 6:33; II Timothy 2:15, and Isaiah 28:10. It's time for us to stop running from the word *Nigger*, and start educating our people and the world of its true identity. What are we afraid of?87

Dr. Laney: Dr. Johnson, can you point out in Scripture how *Niger* means God, King, and Supreme?

Dr. Johnson: Let me reiterate that the term *Niger* is found in Acts 13:1. The word also means Black, along with numerous definitions from one extreme to another. The Hebrew term Ham-Meleck in Jeremiah 36:26 and 38:6 means King. The word *Ham* of Ham-Melech means Black, Negro, Niger or Nigger. The term *Me* of Ham-Melech means Ham or Aham in Sanskrit and Vietnamese. The term *Aham* in Eastern nations means Ham. In Daniel 5:25–26, the term *Me* is linked to the name of God. The word *Le* of Ham-Melech is another Eastern and French word for Homme, which is none other than Hamme or Ham, since the letter *"O"* is exchanged for *"A."* The word *Ch* of Ham-Melech, equals the letters *"I"* and *"C"* which in turn means Aham or Ham.

The term *Negus* in Ethiopia is called King of Kings, and in Hebrew, *Nagas*, means Jesus Ham-Ashiah or Messiah. Isn't Jesus Christ called King of Kings and Lord of Lords, or, may I say, Negus, Niger, or Nigger of Niggers, in Revelation 17:14; 19:16? The word *Negus* is equivalent to the term *Nego*, whereas Nego in Portuguese means Negro. The term Nego in ancient Babylonia meant God. The Hebrew Azariah, a companion of Daniel, was called Abed-Nego, meaning servant of Nego or a Negro.88

Brother Hightower: Dr. Johnson, what other factor substantiate that all utterances, sounds, and every conceivable thought can be traced to one common origin, *Ham, I Am* or *God?*

Dr. Johnson: Every letter of the alphabet means Ham, I Am, or God. The letter *"A"* is an Egyptian symbol for Ox, which the Hindus, Arabs, and Persians called Ham-Za, Ham-Sa, Man, Alif, or One. The Hebrews called *"A,"* "Aleph," and the Greeks, "Alpha," or "Alpham," since *Ha* (the same as He, Him, and Ham) of Alpha means *Ham.* Didn't Jesus call himself Alpha? Before the introduction of vowels by the Greeks, the Egyptians called the Ox, *"Ng,"* which in today's spelling would be Nig, meaning Niger, Nigger, Black, or Ham. The term Ox was called *Am* by the Sumerians, and *Am* means *Ham.* The letter *"B"* is the Egyptian symbol for House, meaning Home, Hame or Ham. The Hebrews called this letter, "Beth." The *"C"* and *"G"* were developed from an Egyptian symbol that represented a boomerang. Both letters were anciently interchangeable and were called Camel, Gimel, and Gamma. Keep in mind that the *"C"* also represents the *"K,"* and the *"K"* for the *"H,"* thereby altering Camel to Kamel or Hamel, meaning Ham. Every letter in every group of Alphabets means Ham.89

Sister Payne: Dr. Johnson, name some other Biblical characters whose names mean Ham.

Dr. Johnson: Samson, Simon, and Samuel are names translated as Ham, since the ancient letter *"S"* was interchangeable with *"H,"* thereby altering their names to Hamson, Himon, and Hamuel. There are other names such as Abednego, Tamar, Thomas. Abednego means servant of a Negro, since *Abed* of Abednego means servant, and *Nego* itself means God or Negro. The term Tamar can be altered to Camar, Kamar, or Hamar, since the ancient letter *"T"* was exchanged for *"C,"* the *"C"* for *"K,"* and the *"K"* for *"H."* Thomas was spelled Chomas, Chamas, Kamas, or Hamas.90

Mr. Jones: Intriguing. Dr. Johnson, how do you know Simon of Cyrene, who carried the Messiah's cross was a Black man when the Bible doesn't call him Black?

Dr. Johnson: In many cases the Bible doesn't apply the word Black to identify Black people. We know that Simon of Cyrene was Black because of the geographical area from whence he came. Remember, Cyrene was located in Northern Africa.

Ms. Dupree: Dr. Johnson, could you describe the remaining letters of the alphabet?

Dr. Johnson: Well, before meeting your request, let me first say that one of the most essential jewels given to the human race was the alphabet which was Divinely inherited through the line of the patriarch Ham. The Ethiopians of Babylon and Africa invented the world's first universal alphabet called cuneiform and hieroglyphic. The Egyptians who learned hieroglyphic from the Ethiopians called this sacred writing "The Words of God."

The Greek alphabet, which was later transmitted to Rome and the British Isles, was invented by the Negro Phoenicians from hieroglyphic. The Negro Phoenicians introduced this alphabet to the Greeks because of their inability to develop their own written language. The Europeans' inability to understand cuneiform and hieroglyphic also prompted the Negroes of Canaan to introduce a simpler alphabet that Europe could comprehend. This was necessary in order to conduct commercial business, curtail verbal agreements, and keep accurate records.91

Mr. Jackson: Dr. Johnson, could you please, as Ms. Dupree has asked, describe the remaining alphabet?

Dr. Johnson: Thank you, Mr. Jackson, I was just about to begin. The letter *"D"* was borrowed from the Negro Egyptians and meant door or entrance. This letter was called *Daleth* by the people of Canaan, and *Delta* by the Greeks. In modern Hebrew, the *"D"* is equal to "R," Re, Ra or Ham. The letter *"E"* was borrowed from the Negro Egyptian picture symbol representing a man rejoicing or shouting. This letter was called *He* (the same as Him or Ham), by the inhabitants of Canaan, *Epsilon* by the Greeks, and *No* by the Assyrians. Keep in mind that the term No was another Ethiopian and Egyptian expression for Amen-Re or Ham.

The letter *"F"* was borrowed from the Negro Egyptian Hieroglyphic, meaning Hook (the same as Ham), by the people of Canaan, and Digamma, Gamma, Camma, Kamma or Hamma by the Greeks. The letter "G" was borrowed from the Negro Egyptian Hieroglyphic (or picture symbol), and represented a boomerang. The inhabitants of Canaan called this letter Hook, Kamel, or Gimel, and the Greeks called it Gamma, which was the same as Camma, Kamma, Hamma or Ham. Keep in mind that the Russian Jewish *"H"* was interchangeable with the Russian *"G."* The letter *"H"* was borrowed from the Negro Egyptians, representing a twisted rope or Ham. The people of Canaan and Syria called this letter *He* or *Ha* which was the same as Him, Ham, Hum, or Hem. The letter *"H"* is one of the four Hebrew letters that make up the name of God known as Tetragrammaton.

The letter *"I"* was borrowed from the Negro Egyptian Hieroglyphic. This letter was called *Yod* by the inhabitants of Canaan, meaning Hand or God. The Greeks called this letter *Iota* or *Kame*, the Hindu called it *A-Ham* or *Ham*. In Old English it is translated as Em, Eme, Unc, Unk, Uncle, or Jesus. The letter *"I"* is also interchangeable with *"C," "Ch"* and *"Y."* The letter *"J"* was borrowed from the Negro Egyptians, and was used to represent a hand presenting a letter. The *"J"* is the Anglo substitution for the Hebrew letter *"Y."* In Arabic it is called Jim (same as Ham), since the Hebrew *"Y"* is also exchanged for *"I"* and the *"I"* for *"C,"* the *"C"* for *"K,"* and the *"K"* for *"H."* The letter *"K"* was borrowed from Negro Egypt and was used to represent the palm of the Hand. The people of Canaan called this letter *Kaph*, the Greeks, *Kappa*, the Assyrians, *Kam*, and the Ethiopians, *House* (the same as Home, Hame or Ham).

The letter *"L"* was borrowed from the Negro Egyptians and it represented a crooked staff or goad. The people of Canaan called this letter *Lamed*, the Greeks, *Lambda*, and the Arabs, *Lam*, which is same as lamb, sheep, or hamal. Keep in mind that the word Hamal is a synonym of Ham. The letters "M" and "N" were borrowed from the Egyptian Hieroglyphic and were originally interchangeable. The letter "M" was called *Mu* by the Greeks, and *Em* (the same as Hem and Ham) by the British. In ancient Egypt and Canaan, the letter *"M"* meant Am or Ham. The Greeks called the *"N," "Nu."* The letter *"O"* was borrowed from the Negro Egyptians and meant Eye or Ra. This letter was called *Ayin* by the people of Canaan, meaning eye. The Greeks called this letter Omicron or Omma. Keep in mind that Omma is the same as Amma, since the letter *"O"* is the same as *"A."*

The word *Amma* means Ham! The letter "P" was borrowed from the Negro Egyptians, and represented the mouth. The Egyptians referred to the mouth as *Re* or *Ra* which meant Ham. The letter *"Q,"* which is equivalent to *"K,"* was borrowed from the Negro Egyptians. The letter *"R,"* borrowed from the Egyptian Hieroglyphic , represented a human head. The people of Canaan called this letter *Res*, (the same as *Ro*), and the Arabs, *Ra*, (the same as Ham). The letter *"S,"* borrowed from the Negro Egyptians, represented a tooth. The ancient letter *"S"* was interchangeable for *"K," "C,"* and *"H."* The people of Canaan called this letter *Shin, Samech,* or *Samekh*, meaning tooth, Cam, or Ham. Let us not overlook that Samech is also spelled Hamech, since the ancient letter *"S"* was interchangeable with *"H."*

The letter "T" was borrowed from the Negro Egyptian Hieroglyphic. The people of Canaan called this cross-shaped letter *Taw* or *Tow*, the Greeks, *Tau*. In modern Hebrew, the *"T"* is Tet. Tet in ancient Egyptian meant Osiris or Ham. The *"T"* was also exchanged for *"K"* and *"C."* The letters *"U," "V," "W," "Y,"* and *"X,"* were borrowed from the Negro Egyptian

Hieroglypic. The people of Canaan called these letters Waw which is the same as Vaw, meaning Hook or Ham. The letter *Waw* or *Vav* is one of the four Hebrew letters (the Tetragrammaton) that make up the name of God. The Greeks and Romans would address Ham as *I Am-Us* or *Ham-Us*, meaning hook, curve, dome, etc. In earlier literature, the letters *"V," "F," "W," "Y,"* and *"U,"* were interchangeable. The *"Z"* was exchanged for *"S,"* and the *"S"* for *"H"* or *"K,"* all of which were translated as Ham.92

Dr. Laney: Dr. Johnson, it seems as though we as a people may never grasp the understanding of our biblical entity. Why is it so hard for some of us to understand these facts?

Dr. Johnson: Dr. Laney, it's not that difficult to understand for those who study and have the power of the Holy Spirit. Just remember Hosea 4:6.

Sister Ford: Dr. Johnson, your book *The Black Biblical Heritage* is definitely a masterpiece. Why did it take you over 25 years to write a book with less than 300 pages? Why so long for such a short book?

Dr. Johnson: Audience, as I have traveled throughout the U.S., I've observed on several occasions that when a non-White author expounds upon his glorious culture, the reaction is quite different than when a White author does the same. The Black author is usually harassed or bullied, mocked or ridiculed, distrusted or doubted, and cross-examined more than any other ethnic group concerning his cultural history.

Sister Ford, for the betterment of Blacks and myself, it was necessary to conduct lengthy research in order to acquire the necessary references to verify the book's authenticity. The Black author, especially the theologian, unlike other scholars, has to

prove nearly every word verbatim before he is fully accepted!
Sister Ford: What is your reasoning as to why Black authors are mistreated in this way?

Dr. Johnson: There are several reasons for such insulting treatment. The very first people to exist on this planet belonged to the Negro race. Negroes developed the origin of thought, the concept of the universe, the world's first sophisticated civilization, and brought forth two other races; the Mongoloids and the Caucasoids. This description alone is the main reason why Black authors are so heavily scrutinized. The two other races are very insistent that such knowledge remain concealed, since they have institutionally reclassified the Negro Egyptians and Ethiopians (children of the Black man Ham), to be Whites.

Melissa: Dr. Johnson, If a person who is half African and half White must take on the identity of a Black, then why can't this same individual, who is as much White as Black, be considered White?

Dr. Johnson: In some section of the globe, many are accepted as Whites, as long as they bear no facial features or any physical resemblance to the Negro race. The only difference in race crossing between Blacks and Whites is that Whites will accept only the whitest of Blacks in their families, rather than the darker ones. On the contrary, Blacks will accept the whitest of Whites as Blacks. The bottom line is that Whites have millions of Blacks in their families. The common practice is to accept Blacks into their families only if the Black's appearance resembles a White's. I personally know several light-skinned Blacks who are members of the KKK, skinheads groups, and the Nazi Party.[93]

Reverend Pierce: Dr. Johnson why is it right to teach Black heritage in our churches?

Dr. Johnson: For several reasons. Mainly because the Prophets recorded our heritage, and have warned us not to become victims of James 2:1–9, by showing respect of persons. By violating such warning, one is subject to becoming a sinner and transgressor! To teach the Bible and deny the existence of one of God's creations, is a sin. Sir, the Holy Spirit will never conceal the truth based upon color. The Scriptures clearly inform us that it is not good to practice this injustice, that God Himself warned us against it. I would rather not be redundant, but remember Hosea 4:6, "My people are destroyed for a lack of knowledge: because thou hast rejected knowledge, I will also reject thee, that thou shalt be no priest to me: seeing thou hast forgotten the law of thy God, I will also forget thy children."

For the Black race to be deprived of this vital information is catastrophic. To teach the Bible and not mention the Black race, is not teaching the whole Bible. It is your duty, sir, to promote the whole truth by recognizing all of God's people, not just a few. By all means, Saints, let's not overlook Matthew 5:15 that warns us not to hide the truth.94

Mr. Higgins: Dr. Johnson, can you furnish us with Bible verses that justify the purpose of this meeting and reflect the nature of your presentation?

Dr. Johnson: The Scripture informs us that before the end of the world, all truth will be known. Matthew 24:14 says, "And this gospel of the kingdom shall be preached in all the world for a witness unto all nations; and then shall the end come." Matthew 10:26 says, "Fear them not, therefore; for there is nothing covered that shall not be revealed; and hidden, that shall not be known."

Mr. Higgins, you're one of many to witness this gathering as merely Bible prophesy, since the truth must be told before the end!95

Mrs. Jones: Dr. Johnson, what are your comments concerning Blacks who believe they're inferior to Whites? What is your solution to this self-destructive problem?

Dr. Johnson: Naturally, this is a false concept based upon the lack of knowing who you are. In reality, every race, in some respect, is inferior and superior to one other. It just so happens that the Black race has been targeted (or may I say by Hollywood, the news media, and other giant industries), to focus only on their mishaps, more than on their successes. The solution to this problem is to self educate. The biblical Job says in a roundabout way, "If I know what you know then how can I be inferior to you?"96
Ms. Gibbes: Dr. Johnson, aside from propoganda, what other factors may have contributed to the belief that Afro-Americans are inferior to other races?

Dr. Johnson: There are reasons despicable beyond one's own imagination. Let me address a major reason that dates back to Adham. It is called "conception indifferences." The early Negro fathers of civilization, who invented philosophy and mathematical sciences, were in total contrast with Euro-thinking. It took savage Europe thousands of years to acquire an elementary understanding of the Black man's high-cultured systems of the ancient world. However, Europeans slowly emerged from the caves of Europe into the civilized world through Socrates, Solon, Plato, Pythagoras, and Aristotle (who were educated in Negro-Egypt), and gradually incorporated Africa's original concept of philosophy and science into their own inferior culture.

The Europeans, other than through war, never fully understood the African science. It was Albert Einstein who actually unraveled some of the African science, and, because of this, was called the greatest scientist who ever lived. Embalming, one of Africa's simplest inventions, still mystifies today's scientists. However, in reference to "conception indifferences," the Europeans (because of their inability to understand, or pronounce African words) started substituting African terms with Greek and Roman names, especially in religion. As a result, their supreme God, Zeus, was noneother than Ham, the father of Cush, whom the Greeks worshiped as Apollo. Cush's son Nimrod was worshiped as Hercules.

In ancient times, Ethiopia, Egypt, Israel, and Greece viewed the color black as sacred and positive since the "Supreme Creator" (life and light) evolved out of darkness. There were other indifferences between Africa and Europe; Blacks read from right to left and perperdicular. The Africans would call Southern Egypt, "Upper Egypt," and Northern Egypt, "Lower Egypt." Looking up was called looking down and vice-versa. No meant yes, and yes meant no. Thumbs up meant death, not mercy. A book's title, introduction, and page one were located in the rear, not in the front of a book.

The Europeans, because of a lack of adaptation, cunningly reverted the universal norm in order to manipulate people of color. They knew that such a maneuver would hinder Black people's performance since their normal ability to perform would be in opposition to the new norms. Europe's next approach was to promote the concept of inferiority, based on Blacks' reluctance to conform to these neo-norms.97

Mr. Todd: Give us an example of one of your "conception indifferences."

Dr. Johnson: Well, let's observe the ancient numerical system where 3-2-1-0 became today's 0-1-2-3. Remember, Adam was born in the year 4000; about 1700 years later, the Great Flood occurred around the year 2300. A little over a 1000 years later Moses was born in the year 1200. It was 200 years later that the Colored King Solomon came to the throne of Israel in the year 1000. This process continued to decrease to the year 1 B.C. Jesus

Ham-Ashiah or Messiah was born about 2 or 3 B.C.E, and lived up to 35 or 36 A.D. Mr. Todd, I hope my answer is satisfactory.

Ms. Dupree: Dr. Johnson, you previously said that all words can be traced to one common origin, "Ham." How would you define Solomon?

Dr. Johnson: The name Solomon was originally spelled Salmon and Zalmon, meaning "dark-skinned man." The prefix Sol of Solomon means Sun. The Greeks called the Sun "Helius," meaning Ham. It is not unusal to call Solomon dark-skinned, since he was a descendant of the Negro race through the Negress Rahab. The Reverend Armistead says: "Solomon was part Negro."[98]

Tim: Dr. Johnson, can you elaborate more on how you know the first man was a Black man?

Dr. Johnson: Sure. This evidence is found in Daniel 7:9. Daniel had a dream of an anthropomorphic figure of God, in the representation of Jesus Christ, with pure wool hair like an African Black man. Some 600 years later, St. John gave a similar description of Jesus by comparing His hair to wool, and His feet to fine brass as if burned in a furnace.

Tim, the Egyptian word for brass is the same as copper since brass is manufactured from copper. This word is pronounced, "Kam," meaning Ham or Black. *Webster's Third New International Dictionary* identifies a black copper called melaconite. This image of God in a humanoid form with Negro features was perpetual since God always existed. This Negroid depiction of God was in existence long before the creation of Adham and Eve. From archeological research, man has been proven to have originated on the Africa Continent.[99]

Mr. Higgins: Dr. Johnson, there are individuals who measure success solely based on their occupational social status. What are your comments?

Dr. Johnson: Well, let me quote the 12th-Century Catholic priest St. Barnard: "To know the height of the heaven, the width of the earth, the depth of the sea, and know not from whence you came, is like a person with no foundation. To participate in other activites without knowing who you are, is a waste of energy." That person, says Barnard, will never build buildings, but create a world of ruins. If we could name of all the stars of the universe, and know not who we are, then we have failed!100

Pastor Edwards: Dr. Johnson name one great difference between Afro-Americans and Africans.

Dr. Johnson: We have money and they have honor; something that money can never buy. Afro-Americans have so much White in their countenance or way of thinking, that their future, without a doubt, is on the brink of doom; a course that Africa will certainly avoid!

Melissa: Dr. Johnson, I believe that Africans will avoid the course of destruction because of their understanding of God and themselves.

Dr. Johnson: A lot of people share this opinion. The average African style of worship seems to keep them in harmony with the universe and their Creator; a virtue that Black Americans are rapidly losing, primarily because we invest too much time and money in materialism rather Spiritualism.

Dr. Laney: Dr. Johnson, you have suggested dozens of books and references to support the presence of Blacks in the Bible. What are some of the manipulations we should be aware of while researching our Black Biblical Heritage, or secular history?

Dr. Johnson: Interesting question, because there are untold numbers of tricks and games in nearly every book I've read concerning Black history; especially the new revised bibles which seem to reveal only bits and pieces. It appears that all subjects pertaining to Black history are minimized, and that only 20% of the truth revealing any Afro subject is revealed. To deprive a people of 80% of their most valuable history is surely a devastation to one's morale and self-esteem.

Sad to say, it appears that most scholars have primarily represented Blacks in the area of crime and inferiority. How unfortunate! To focus more on your question, I believe we should become more aware of words that are said to be obsolete, since many of these words shed considerable light on the history of Black people. Let me give you an example. The obsolete term *Kyngham*, is now replaced by the word *Kingdom*. My point is to alert you to the suffix *ham* of Kyngham. *Ham* is a synonym of *dom*.

There is also a practice of using deceptive terms in biblical phrases, such as the description of Moses' Ethiopian wife Zipporah who, in some new translations, is called an Abysinian instead of an Ethiopian. My point is that the average Bible reader wouldn't associate the Arabic term Abysinia with Africa as they would with Ethiopia. Another deception is the portrayal of Ethiopians and Egyptians as Caucasians, which is ludicrous, since they were descendants of Ham who was Negro.

Let me continue. There is the practice of anagrams; for example, in the Hebrew Kabbalah God is called Mah. Mah in reverse is Ham, the very name we're reminded to resent. We should also observe that all vowels are interchangeable so that the spelling Ham is also Hem, Him, Hom, Hum, Hym, etc. Let us also recognize that the ancient consonants were also interchangeable. The ancient letter *"S"* was exchanged for *"H,"* thereby altering Sam to Ham. Last, but not least, on most American maps of the world, Africa, which is three times the size of the United States, is drawn smaller than its actual size.101

Brother Tidwell: Dr. Johnson, you mentioned that we should be cautious of the new revised bibles. What should we be cautious of?

Dr. Johnson: You should be cautious of the sneaky exploitations and distortions of the Black race found in those revised books. The old *King James Version Bible*, not *The New King James Bible,* published in 1979, is about the best Bible to study in relation to your culture and salvation. If you think I'm exaggerating, then take a *King James Version Bible*, published before 1979, and compare the following verses with those in other revised bibles: Job 30:30; Song of Solomon 1:5–6; Daniel 7:9, 10:6 and Revelation 1:14–15. These verses, written between 325 A.D. and 1611 A.D., were the last ones to have survived the great conspiracy to wipe out any evidence of an early African presence. The new revised bibles have finally accomplished this goal, as evidenced by Blacks saying, "What difference does it make?"

Mr. Todd: Dr. Johnson, what is so important about 325 A.D. through 1611 A.D.?

Dr. Johnson: During the year 325 A.D., the Byzantine Emperor, Constantine, commanded 219 bishops throughout the empire to convene in Turkey. This meeting was held for several reasons; to redefine religion, eliminate certain books of the Bible, (especially those books that reflected any hints of an African origin of Christianity), and to use religion as a tool for government. This meeting was called the Nicene Council or Conference. The conspirational ideas of the Nicene Council remained in place through the reign of King James, who authorized the *King James Version Bible*, a Bible that had a few remaining Scriptures pertaining to a Black presence. As I have previously stated, the new revised bibles have delivered the final blow by eliminating the remaining key Scriptures that present an early African presence!102

Bishop Franklin: Dr. Johnson, where are these books today that were excised from the Bible?

Dr. Johnson: Many of these books are still found in the Greek Septuagent, Latin Vulgate, and Catholic Bibles. The Dead Sea Scrolls, which contain all the books of the Bible plus an additional 15 books called the Apocrypha, are located in the Jerusalem Museum.

Bishop Franklin: Dr. Johnson, after we have received the Holy Spirit which guides us to spread the word of God, in addition to saving many souls, what would you consider our next objective? What other critical changes should we seek in order to free ourselves from the social yoke?

Dr. Johnson: Naturally we should strive for salvation and strength through our Lord Jesus Christ. After obtaining these sources, we should then commence to battle evil. The first social yoke we should confront and obliterate, is the Western lie concerning the word *Niger* or *Nigger*. As long as Blacks continue to hate and dodge the word *Niger,* never realizing its sacred definition as God, King, and Supreme, we'll never leap beyond our boundaries, but continue to remain in chaotic ignorance! It is a tragedy that Blacks have allowed Caucasians to take an ancient Holy word that meant God, and revert this word to a weapon against people of color!

Pastor Edwards: Dr. Johnson, society (especially our people) has been socially trained to respond harshly upon hearing the word

Niger or Nigger. Many have angrily perceived this word as offensive or derogative. Now, sir, are you telling the audience that the word Niger doesn't bother you when heard?

Dr. Johnson: Absolutely not, since I know both who I am and the original definition of Nigger. Pastor Edwards, I've learned to turn anger into positive energy through the power of the Holy Spirit. Ever remembering Romans 12:19 which says, "Vengeance is mine, I will repay, saith the Lord." My credence is that sticks and stones may break my bones but words will never hurt me. As a people of "The Supreme Creator" we must exhibit tenacity and courage, always realizing that the Holy Spirit will never allow a people to become subjective to or controlled by any word other than the true name of God. The only word in the universe that possesses the megaton effect on man's ears, mind, and heart like a hydrogen bomb that leaves its victims in a traumatic paralytic state, is none other than the true name of God.

We must understand that one of God's many names means *Truth,* and that *Truth*, according to the Scriptures, will painfully cut us like a two-edged sword. Now when we hear the terms Jehova, Yahwe, Idonia, God, Allah, etc., why don't these names immediately deliver as similar a jolting effect upon the human psyche as the word *Niger?* My question is why does the word *Niger* overpower the ultimate effect of the word God if the word itself doesn't mean God? Didn't the Hebrews call God *Elo-him*? The term *him* of Elo-him means Ham, since the ancient letter *"I"* was interchangeable with *"A."* Doesn't the word *Ham* means Black, Niger, or Negro? The term *El Shaddai* means God-Shad, God-Shade, God-Dark, God-Black, God-Niger, or God-Negro, since the Canaanite El means God, and Shad is a translation of Shade or Shadow. The word Dai of El Shaddai means Day, since the letter *"I"* is exchanged for *"Y."* The first definition of Day meant dark or black, since the first Day was evening and morning, indicating darkness or blackness.

God is referred to as a shadow in Psalm 91:1. There is also the shadow of Peter in Acts 5:15 that heals the sick. Doesn't the term *Omnipotent* mean "God Almighty?" *Om* of Omnipotent means Him, which in turn means Ham, Black, Niger, or Negro. The term *Ni* of *Omnipotent* was anciently called "Our Lord" by the Ethiopian-Babylonians, and "God" by the Negro-Egyptians. Remember, the term *Ni* is equal to Na, Ne, No, Nu, and Ny, since all vowels are interchangeable.

The Hebrews called God "No'Am (Ham)- YHVH" and "Nothing." The name "No" or "No'A" was also applied to Ham, the Deity of the ancient Ethiopians and Egyptians. After observing these facts, why is it difficult to understand that God's true name is Niger or Ham? Didn't God called Himself "I Am?"
The letter *"I"* of I Am was anciently exchanged for *"C"* or *"Ch,"* the *"C"* or *"Ch"* for *"K"* or *"Kh,"* and the *"K"* for *"H,"* thereby altering I Am to Cam, Cham, Kam, Kham, Ham, Black, Niger, or Negro. Pastor Edwards, the importance of a word is how you understand it. I believe a person shouldn't publicly use terms if they lack understanding of the meaning. My fellow brethren, it's not what people say about you, it's how you react.[103]

Dr. Carey: Dr. Johnson, I must agree with you that the Hebrew, Latin, French, and most European Bibles begin the spelling of Ham's name with *"Ch"* and *"C,"* whereas ancient historians began the spelling with the letter *"K"* or *"Kh."*

Reverend Jason: Dr. Johnson, I personally believe we should only apply the titles Black and Afro-American to identify our people, and no longer call ourselves Colored, Negroes or Nigers, because of the stigma of those terms.

Dr. Johnson: Well, it's definitely one's own right to choose the name of their choice. But I've always believed it's not the name that makes a people but the people behind the name. Changing a race title will never win a person an ounce of freedom since freedom only comes from the acknowledgment of God or Truth. Remember John 8:32, "Ye shall know the truth and the truth shall make you free." The truth manifests courage to oppose evil, which in due time brings about love, peace, and harmony.

Let us not overlook the fact that the names Jew and Christian were once viewed by the heathens as racial titles. Yet, the Jews never altered their identity to please their adversaries, but, instead, accepted these titles as a symbol of honor, and went on about their business; a discipline that Blacks have yet to learn. Reverend Jason, there's nothing in a name but the people who wear it!104

Brother Hightower: Dr. Johnson, what could a person or race gain by allowing others to publicly insult them with racial slurs?

Dr. Johnson: We have a heavy responsibility facing us that can only be handled by using weapons within. We must always choose moral solutions over physical confrontations. Let's face it, if the Holy Spirit is rooted in our souls, as we profess, then why do we allow sick people to arouse us? What happens to our God wisdom, strength, and temperance? Why do we permit others to possess such control over our emotions?

I believe once we unite as Christians against misunderstood words such as *Niger* (or any other terms which we've been Westernly coached to misinterpret), we will definitely silence the antagonist. Let's be strategic; the only mental weapon the antagonist has over Black people is his ability to manipulate us with the word *Niger*. The antagonist can only be deactivated when Blacks, through God, take complete charge of their own lives and exhibit a mental/spiritual resistance against the antagonist's assaults, along with totally ignoring the antagonist's misinterpretation of the word *Niger*.

But if Blacks can't spiritually break away from this man-eating octopus, then, as previously stated, we have another 100 years to go. Such maneuvers toward reviving our worth to God is one of many avenues to happiness. Why are we, who were the world's first spiritualists, so conscious about what others think of us? Why do we confess in our churches that God is our shield, but diminish upon hearing the word *Niger*? Why do we allow the very people who built their Western civilizations from the ideas of our own ancient foreparents, to possess such great control over us? I believe that as Christian Black people we should question ourselves, in the name of God and the Holy Spirit, as to why we allow ourselves to be that vulnerable. Listen saints, there are grown adults over nintey years of age who will cry like a baby on hearing the word *Niger*. Now isn't that a disgrace for a Christian who is supposed to be shielded by God? Blacks will shout every Sunday that nothing is impossible with God, but, when hearing the word *Niger*, will cry mercifully to the law. Now if that's not hypocrisy then what is? Wake up and read the handwriting on the wall, saints. We have blindly allowed the Caucasian to take the ancient, sacred word *Niger* or *Nigger* and use it as a weapon against us.

Mrs. Richardson: What necessary steps should we take to endure and understand the true meaning of any racial terms?

Dr. Johnson: There are many, but heed the Scriptures that inform us to pray and study, and encourage our teachers to do the same, because man's strongest strength exists in the word of God, and with this belief we shall prevail!

The great American writer Horace Greeley stated, "It is mentally and socially impossible to enslave a Bible reading people." Now, are we a Bible reading people? Let us not overlook Proverbs

3:5–6 as the Colored King Solomon says, "Trust in the Lord with all thine heart and do not depend upon your own understanding. In all your ways, trust in God and He will direct your path." My fellow brethren, the most difficult thing for a Christian is to do the right thing! Our message or intention may be right, but let us make sure that we've chosen the right methods to solve our problems. Once we have discoveded the disease, let us be assured we've selected the right cure. We can endure racism by raising the level of our consciousness of who we are through God-Hama-Kom. Wake up!105

Tim: Dr. Johnson what other drawbacks must we overcome?

Dr. Johnson: Tim, there are many obstacles we must confer with. One is to stop wanting people to befriend or like us, and, instead, respect us! To accomplish this task involves knowing God-Hama-Kom. This would definitely set our people on a new course of identity.

Tim: Dr. Johnson I'm only 10 years old and I want people to like me.

Dr. Johnson: Tim, most of us share that same desire, but respect is greater!

Melissa: Dr. Johnson, what can we do as a people to stop the hatred against us?

Dr. Johnson: Melissa, Whites around the world seem to imitate Black people in many fashions; music, dance, style of walk, dressing, hiptalking, slang, males wearing earrings, pants hanging below the buttocks, sunbathing to acquire a darker skin color, visiting beauty parlors to have curls pressed in their hair, and many other ways. The hatred and crime against Blacks will universally decrease when the Black man learns to stop hating and killing himself. When he has accomplished this moral example, believe it or not, the rest of the world will follow accordingly. We must lead the way!

Melissa: Dr. Johnson, I believe there is hope along with additional blessings for our people if we try harder.

Dr. Johnson: I agree. There is an abundance of hope, but remember hope is like the air we breathe; if we cease to apply it, then we'll perish as a people. The idea of hope is like truth; it must be put into practice, because we can't love unless we hope, nor hope unless we have knowledge.

Melissa: Dr. Johnson, why do our people reject pictures of God, Jesus and other biblical characters as Blacks?

Dr. Johnson: Simple; because we have been brainwashed to resent our own appearances. We find it quite difficult to praise what we have been taught to despise! Even though the Bible plainly describes God and Jesus as having dark complexions and wool hair, we still prefer to exclude this crucial information from our conscience. Melissa, as previously stated, it has been systematically instilled in Blacks to deny a Black Biblical Heritage. How sad![106]

Reverend Jason: Dr. Johnson, at this very hour as we speak, what should we socially reach out for (other than what we've already expressed) in attempting to uplift our people?

Dr. Johnson: That has to be Divinely accomplished in the name of Jesus Ham-Ashiah or Messiah. Remember Matthew 6:33; "But seek ye first the kingdom of God, and his righteousness; and all things shall be added unto you." Again, do not overlook Hosea 4:6; "My people are destroyed from a lack of knowledge." My brethren, we do not need any more athletes, entertainers, or comedians, but rather an army of religious scholars to reeducate our people and the rest of the world about who we are. We need to emphasize to our youth the need to apply their minds in the area of scholastics, rather than their arms, legs, and backs in the field of sports. We need more scientists, writers, and inventors, not athletes, actors, and comedians!

If we don't change this direction, then history will surely record us as no more than a people of entertainers. That's not a very bright picture for a people who developed the world's first civilizations, philosophy, and mathematical sciences. Let the world praise us for our mental power, not back power. If we seek world attention then let us achieve it through the channels of education. Saints, shouldn't we be reminded that great civilizations are not built by athletes and comedians, nor are judicial systems controlled by them?

Mrs. Jones: Dr. Johnson, I am troubled about "Black History Month" receiving national attention in the coldest and shortest month of the year. Whoever chose February to honor Black history, must have gotten up on the wrong side of the bed.

Dr. Johnson: Believe it or not, February was chosen by our government. I'd rather not go into detail, sensing it will misdirect the program's main topic. However, I do share your concerns, and believe our history should be discussed 365 days a year, instead of 28 days in the cold month of February. If we can expound on Jewish and Caucasian history for 12 months, then surely we should give our own history equal respect; a respect which is vital to our survival as a people. We spend only 10% out of a year studying our heritage, and 90% studing Jewish and Caucasian history.

Pastor Edwards: So you view learning the history of our people to be the primary solution to our sustained survival?

Dr. Johnson: Indeed, since our people were the first to write history and the Bible. I believe that spiritual and natural knowledge are the delivering sources toward salvation. I perceive knowledge as a road map and compass, helping man to reach his destiny. That knowledge can help us understand what was and what will be, and those who lack spiritual and social knowledge will lack spiritual and social gains. By having knowledge of ourselves, we will be able to understand others, since mankind is derived from the African race, which, through the guidance of the Supreme Creator, pioneered the world in various new fields of arts, science, philosophy, physics, liberal arts, religion and metaphysics.

I believe that a people without knowledge of itself is like a tree without roots, and once we understand not only the American history, but our African history as well, we will certainly be able to grasp a broader view of where the European culture derived.107

Pastor Edwards: Dr. Johnson, you actually believe Moses was Black?

Dr. Johnson: Oh, without a doubt, his ancestry was of the Negro race.

Reverend Jason: Dr. Johnson could you be a little more explicit about how the word *Niger* or *Nigger* originally meant God, King, or Supreme?

Dr. Johnson: There are several explanations, but let me first focus upon the Egyptian word *Kim* or *Kam* which the Hebrews later adopted as Cham, Ham, or Am. As earlier stated, the name anciently meant "extremely black," and was translated Negro, Niger, or Nigger. The name Ham, from its earlier use, was always applied to a head of state, God, or King. The Ethiopians, Egyptians, and even the Semites, for many centuries, worshiped

Ham as a God! His name still remains prominent in every aspect of today's religion.

The name Ham, to signify authority, has been used throughout all cultures and Bibles as a prefix, infix, and suffix. The word *Ham-Melech, Ham-Ashiah, Ham-Masiah, Ham-Elehk, Ham-Ahiah, Ham-Massiah,* or *Ham-Melek* is the Hebrew root word for the Greek term Messiah; a truth that most preachers and missionaries will choke with a smile before admitting.

Now the Ethiopian word *Negus,* which the Hebrews called Nagas, means "King of Kings." Remember, Jesus Christ in Revelation 17:14 and 19:16 is called "King of Kings" and "Lord of Lords." The term *Negus* is equivalent to the word Nego which means Negro, Black, Niger, or Nigger! There is other evidence as God is addressed as *Eloham, Hama-Kom,* and *Ha-Ra-Ham-An,* whereas the Savior is addressed as Jesus Ham-Ashiah, the same as Jesus Messiah.

God and Jesus both referred to themselves as *I Am,* the same as Ham, Black, or Niger, since the ancient letter *"I"* of *"I Am"* was exchanged for *"C"* or *"Ch,"* the *"C"* or *"Ch"* for *"K"* or *"Kh,"* and the *"K"* or *"Kh"* for *"H,"* thereby altering *I Am* to *Cam, Cham, Kam, Kham,* or Ham. Jesus' blood of communion is called Niger or Nigger, since blood is called Hem, Hema- Hemoglobin, or Hamoglobin. Finally, Jesus called Himself the Bread of Life. Bread in Hebrew is pronounced *Ham.*

My objective is to expose the great Euro-lie regarding the name Ham. The very word we're drilled to scorn or despise actually means God and Jesus.108

Mrs. Lott: Dr. Johnson, I've noticed that you've put a lot of the blame for Black ignorance on our churches, but what about the congregation that fails to demand knowledge?

Dr. Johnson: It is the minister's responsibility to make his people aware of all biblical truth, whether they demand it or not. The ministers of all people should know that the Holy Spirit never buries truth based upon color! John 16:13 tells the ministers that the Spirit of God will guide him in all truth and show him things to come. It is the minister's duty to work in accordance with this verse, realizing that all truth is not sweet to hear.

Hebrews 4:12 informs the ministers that truth will cut us like a two-edged sword. The ministers must enforce the concept that we have two forms of truth; the bitter and sweet. Not merging these truths deprives us of having the whole truth.

Mrs. Lott: Again Dr. Johnson, clarify your reasoning of why you believe ministers duck truth based on color.

Dr. Johnson: Let me first repeat that all ministers do not fit this mold. We have a few ministers who are totally color-blind and will teach and lay their lives on the line for any form of truth or justice. But, of course, we have more than our share who will not; ministers who will only promote half of the truth to avoid rocking the boat. Let us be reminded, that the truth comes in two forms; sweet and bitter. Naturally, it's the bitter truth, in reference to Hebrews 4:12, that generates disturbance. For the world to openly admit that the very people they resent are the true heroes of the Bible would undoubtedly rock the boat, causing a world uproar!

Now in reference to your question, many of our public figures are still in search of who they are, and, thereby, find it quite difficult to expound on a subject they view as offensive, or know little about. I strongly believe their reason for ducking this subject is solely based upon fear and self-denial, which doesn't comply with II Timothy 1:7 that says "For God hath not give us the spirit of fear, but of power, and of love, and of a sound mind." Many of our public figures are still in debate about whether to remain socially indentured or become spiritually led! I would like to reiterate that a devotee of God will never intentionally duck Scriptures based upon race or color. So my final comment to your question is; are these ministers loyal to the work God-Hama-Kom assigned them?

Ms. Dupree: Dr. Johnson, will you give this group a detailed description of Jesus' Negro genealogy?

Dr. Johnson: Jesus Ham-Ashiah, or Messiah, was a pure man in the Spirit of God, but not genetically, since He was of Ham's descent as well as Shem's. Jesus' great-great-great grandmother was a Black woman named Rahab the Canaanite, a descendant of the Negro Ham through Canaan. Following Israel's departure from Negro-Egypt, under the leadership of Moses, Rahab the Negress met a Jew by the name of Salmon. They later married and had a son named Boaz, who fathered Obed. Obed begot Jesse, Jesse begot David, and David begot the Colored King Solomon, from whom descended Jesus Ham-Ashiah.

Jesus' genealogy is also traced to the Negress Jezebel through her daughter Athaliah, who married a Judean King named Jehoram. They had a son named Ahaziah, whose offpring continued that Hamitic line up to the Messiah Christ. I would like to also stress that the Hebrews were a mixed people before and after departing Negro-Egypt. Remember, Genesis 41:45, 50–52 and 46:20, speak of the Hebrew Joseph, while living in Egypt, marrying and having children from the Negress-Egyptian, Asenath. The priest Ezra in Ezra 9:2 says, "For they have taken of their daughters for themselves, and for their sons: so that the Holy Seed have mingled themselves with the people of those lands: yea, the hand of the princes and rulers hath been chief in this trespass."

Race mixing was widely practiced, even among Hebrew leaders such as Abraham, David, and Solomon. Ezekiel 16:3 informs us that God-Eloham reminded the Hebrews of their genetic mixture with the Negro Canaanites; "And say, thus saith the Lord God unto Jerusalem: Thy birth and nativity is of the land of Canaan, thy father was an Amorite, and mother a Hittite." Keep in mind that the Amorites and Hittites were Negro children of Ham through Canaan.109

Pastor Edwards: Dr. Johnson, during your introduction you told us that Jesus, in Revelation 3:14, is called Amen, and that the term anciently meant Ham, the same as Ammon, Amon or Amon-Re, the Sun-God of Egypt. Can you be a little more specific in your description?

Dr. Johnson: The name Amen, the same as Jesus, Ammon, Amon, or Amen-Re, can be spelled Hamen or Hamon, the same as Ham, since *Am* of Amen is an alternative form of Ham. In some ancient cultures the letter *"H"* was silent, and because of this was eliminated from words. Let me give you some examples; honor, honest, hour, heir, hombre, and homage, are words pronounced without the sound of *"H."* Well, in some ancient nations these same words would have been spelled as pronounced, without the letter *"H."* However, in today's Bible the words Amad, Amal, Amalek, Amasa, Amasai, Ami, Amber, Ammah, Ammi, Ammiel, Ammihud, Ammishaddai, Amminadab, Ammisabad, Ammon, Amon, and Amram, were anciently spelled with an *"H."* The term Amen was no exception!110

Mr. Gibbes: Dr. Johnson, are there any other words, besides the word Niger, that we are conditioned to perceive as derogative, when in reality the word itself means "Holy?"

Dr. Johnson: Several. The word *Sambo* was worshiped throughout Asia for centuries. Most names given to the American slaves were names that were anciently praised as Gods and Goddesses, such as Tom, whom was none other than the Negro King Nimrod, the worshiped God-Deity of Babylon. The name Thomas is a derivative of Tom, meaning Ham, since the ancient letter *"T"* was exchanged for *"C,"* the *"C"* for *"K"* and the *"K"* for *"H,"* thereby altering Thomas to Chomas or Chamas, Khomas or Khamas, and Hhomas or Hhamas. These were also spelled Hham and Kham.

Another biblical name believed to be derogative is Jemima, or Jemimah, the daughter of Job, who is biblically described along with her sisters, as the most beautiful women of their era. We may best recognize the name Jemima by the name "Aunt Jemima," a Black woman on corn meal and pancake containers. Black people have been so well-tricked that it's embarrassing!111

Mr. Coolidge: Dr. Johnson, comment on the Anglo myth of the Black man only being three-fifths of a man.

Dr. Johnson: This is a fabrication that should affect Blacks no more than any other fairy tale. It is a biblical and archeological fact that the first human on earth was a Black man. This constitutes him as an original or whole man, who later produced fractions, or other races. The Black man (the original blueprint of mankind), being stigmatized as being three-fifths of a man, is one of the most ridiculous stories I've ever encountered. When you say Adam you're saying God-Ham, God-Black, God-Niger, or God-Nigger, since *Ad* of Adam means God, and *Am* of Adam indicates Ham. Remember, *Am* is equivalent to Ham, and anciently Adam was spelled Adham. Audience, the three-fifths myth is a simple form of reverse psychology!112

Dr. Laney: Dr. Johnson, where in the U.S. Constitution does it identify Blacks or Afro-Americans as three-fifths?

Dr. Johnson: It is found in article one, section three.

Dr. Carey: Dr. Johnson, I can honestly say that in nearly every old biblical text I've researched, the name Ham has always represented a curse and Black people. However, in the most recent publications and movies, Ham is redefined and portrayed as a White man. Could you comment on this sudden shift?

Dr. Johnson: Sure. The message is clear. The world doesn't mind promoting the truth concerning Ham's color as long as Black people remain tricked by the Western myth that Ham's color represents a curse. However, as Blacks around the globe are beginning to awaken from this subterfuge, with pride in their complexion, realizing that the majority of people in the world and the Bible resemble their race, has brought about a new change. They are beginning to see that the same people who confess to hate dark skin, support a trillion dollar industry that produces various products designed to acquire the Black man's complexion. Such awareness has definitely compelled today's Bible institutions to reclassify Ham from Black to White. This is not as bad as our Black preachers lying back saying, "what difference does it make."

The Confederate President Jefferson Davis, during one of his great speeches regarding secession of states, plainly indicated the Black as a son of Ham. The truth of Ham being Black was heavily preached from the dawn of history to the late 1960s A.D.113

Mr. Gibbes: Dr. Johnson, how would you comment on whites harrassing Afro-Americans to go back to Africa?

Dr. Johnson: I would tell Whites to set the example by first returning to Europe. Africa isn't a bad place; in Matthew 2:13–14, Eloham instructed Joseph to take Jesus the Savior and Mary to reside there. Remember Hosea 11:1?

Mr. Gibbes: Dr. Johnson, what was Africa originally called?

Dr. Johnson: Ham. Then later Africa adopted other titles such as Akebulan, Ethiopia, Libya, Kemite, the same as Egypt, Olympia, and Sudan.114

Mr. Coolidge: Dr. Johnson, can you give us a description of the similarities between America and Africa?

Dr. Johnson: Both continents were adjoined during the Pangaea period and were first inhabited by the Negro race since the Eastern and American Indians are genetically children of Ham. I would like to also stress that the name America is translated as Africa or Ham, since the prefix *Am* of America means Ham. *Ame* of America also means Ham or Hame, since Ame too is spelled Hame or Ham. The infix *Ri* of America, is noneother than Re or Ra, the Sun God of Egypt, who was known as Ham. The suffix *Ca* of America is the same as Ka or Ha, since the ancient letter *"C"* was exchanged for *"K,"* and the *"K"* for *"H,"* also meaning Ham.115

Dr. Carey: Dr. Johnson, you mentioned Moses was anciently called Niger, which you've explained throughout this program to mean God, King, and Supreme. What further evidence can you offer to support this claim?

Dr. Johnson: Moses, Mose, Mosheh, Moshei, Mozes, Mohr, etc., was also called Cushman. The word *Cush* of Cushman anciently meant Black or Niger, referring to Ethiopia! Naturally, *Man* of Cushman means Homo, and Homo means Hama or Ham, since the letter *"O"* is exchanged for *"A."* Moses was also called "Mor" or "Moor," which meant Schwartz, Negri, Negro, Niger, or Black in ancient times. Afro-Americans have little understanding of these terminologies, and have been so well tricked regarding their heritage, until I personally have laughed to keep from crying!116

Elder Benson: Dr. Johnson, name other characters in the Bible that we highly praise, whose name means Nigger or Niger?

Dr. Johnson: Let me remind the audience that all sounds and conceivable thoughts are traced to one common origin; *"I Am,"* which is the same as Ham. Now in reference to your question, Abraham's, Issac's and Jacob's names, even to this day mean "God," "Niger" or "Nigger." The term Abraham is merely the expression "Father Ham-Ham," or "Father Sun Ham," since *Ab* of Abraham is a Negro-Ethiopian Babylonian word meaning Father, and *Ra* of Abraham was none other than Egypt's Sun-God, Ham. *Ham* itself means all of the above.

The name Issac itself means Chaim, Chaem, Cham, or Ham, since Ham means Cham, Chiam, Chaem, Chaim and Isaac. The shortened form of Isaac happens to be the word "Is" or "Iss." The term "Is" happens to be the word "As" or " Ass." Doesn't the Biblical term Ass means Ham-Or, which is none other than Ham? Wasn't Ham also called *Or?* The term "Is" also means man, and doesn't man mean Homo, the same as Hama or Ham, since the letter *"O"* is exchanged for *"A?"*

Last but not least, the name Jacob means James, Jim, Jam, Ham, Yam, Black, or Niger. The Hebrew letter *"Y"* is the Anglo-Saxon's *"J,"* thereby altering James, Jim, and Jam to Yames, Yim and Yam. Didn't the ancient Arabs call Ham, "Yam," and the letter *"Y"* of Yam was also interchangeable with *"I,"* thereby transforming Yam to I Am? The Old German name for Jacob was "Ya-Niger" or "God-Niger," since *Ya* of "Ya-Niger" means Yah or God. Naturally, Niger means Ham or God. In Old German Jacob was also called "Hok-Ham," Now in respect to James, the name is also an Old Gaelic form of Hamish, and a Spanish form of Dago, Diago, Diego, or Niger.117

Elder Benson: Dr. Johnson, could you be a little more specific regarding the word Dago meaning Nigger or Niger?

Dr. Johnson: Sure. The term Diago, or Dago, is a Spanish word meaning James, and, as earlier stated, the name James is also spelled Jam, whereas Jam is Yam since the Hebrew letter *"Y"* is the Anglo's *"J."* Ham, as a Black man, was called Yam by the Arabs!

Mrs. Jefferson: Dr. Johnson, what about the biblical Noah?

Dr. Johnson: The name Noah also means Cham, Chiam, Chaim, Haim, Hiam, Heim, Hame, Ham, Negro, Black, Niger, or Nigger.118

Mrs. Richardson: What about Benjamin?

Dr. Johnson: The name Benjamin is also called Himi-Ni which is the same as Hami-Ni, since the letters *"I"* and *"A"* are interchangeable, and Ni, the same as No, also means Ham.119

Pastor Edwards: Dr. Johnson, why have people of color been consistently lectured to totally despise the name of Ham?

Dr. Johnson: Simple; because within the name Ham exists every thread of Power and Truth. The very name itself means I Am, God, Yahwe, Jehova, Adonia, Eloham, Elohim, Hama-Kom, El Shaddai, The Most High, Self Existence, Self Sufficient, Perfect, Freedom, Infinity, Eternity, Immutability, Omnipotence, Omniscience, Omnipresence, Emmanuel, Messiah, Savior, Ham-Ashiah, Christ, Jesus, Anointed One, Prince of Peace, The Good Shepard, Justice, Love, Mercy, Grace, etc. The name Ham is the very essence of man's beginning, present, and future. The term Ham is the molecularity of all entity of existence.

Pastor Edwards: Why would you say the name Ham is the very essence of the beginning and the molecularity of all fabrics of existence?

Dr. Johnson: Pastor Edwards, that's not hard to understand when acknowledging the name "I Am" is none other than Ham, Elohim, or Eloham! Sincerely sir, we don't need a Ph.D. to figure that out.

Reverend Jason: And what molecularity are you speaking of?

Dr. Johnson: The very air you breathe was anciently called Ham or Cham. The Greeks would refer to air, as "A-Emi." Keep in mind that the letter *"A"* stands "Alpha," and Emi for Ham or Ami. Didn't the ancient term "Or" mean air, and wasn't Ham called Or? The term Kam-Sin, or Ham-Sin, means a very hot wind that blows from the Sahara to Egypt and Israel. Remember, the word Kamil-Kaze means the Divine Wind. Let it be acknowledged that the Egyptian word *Ox* of oxygen meant Ng, Am, or Ham. Water in the ancient world was pronounced Yam and Yom, and didn't the Arabs call Ham, "Yam?" The blood in our veins is called Hem, Hemo, and Hamoglobin. Last but not least, the Hebrews called bread, "Ham." Again, I could go on and on.[120]

Ms. Louis: Dr. Johnson, throughout this program, you have defined and deciphered many words, now could you do the same with the word color?

Dr. Johnson: That's quite interesting because the prefix of color anciently meant "The Black God of the rain." The suffix *"Or"* meant Ham and Lord.[121]

Melissa: Dr. Johnson, you have named numerous biblical characters whose names mean dark or black. Can you name others?

Dr. Johnson: Well, the name of Nehemiah's father, Hachaliah, meant dark. Saul's father, Kish or Cis, meant black, a name derived from the word Cush, Kush, or Ethiopia. The name Kedar, the son of Ishmael, meant "black skinned man. Let us also remember, that black is defined as "very very dark."122

Ms. Dupree: Dr. Johnson, you previously addressed Paul as a dark-looking man. What color was his great teacher Gamaliel?

Dr. Johnson: Naturally, every native of the Mediterranean coast was a dark or black-skinned person. Let me also mention Gamaliel's name, which is also spelled Hamaliel, since the Slavic Jewish letter *"H"* is equivalent to *"G."*123

Mrs. Pinkham: Dr. Johnson, why should we continue to look upon the past?

Dr. Johnson: Because we are a product of the past which makes our present and future. Doesn't our Bible remind us to remember the past, since it holds the key to the kingdom of heaven? Should we discard our Christian beliefs because the practice began nearly 2000 years ago? Absolutely not! The Israelis have honorably spend millions of dollars annually to remind the world of their experiences; from slavery in Negro-Egypt to the holocaust in Nazi Germany. The Afro-Americans, who are presently dragging their feet, are the only race in the world to be harrassed about their heritage and their desire to have freedom.124

Tim: Dr. Johnson, what Scriptures prove that the Negro race once ruled the planet before any others?

Dr. Johnson: Well, getting to the very base of your question, the earliest Scriptures are located in Genesis 2:7, 19–24, and describe the creation of the first man, Adam. Keep in mind that the name Adam or Adham means Man, Homo, Hama or Ham. The ancients often defined Adam as being dark-red black earth. Wasn't Adam made in the image of God-Eloham, or Elohim, and in Daniel 7:9 and 10:6, wasn't God described as having pure wool hair and dark skin? Tim, this description of God is a striking resemblance to the appearance of your biological father.

Another account of the Black man's rule is found in Genesis 10:8–12, involving the Ethiopian Nimrod, the world's first King and mighty hunter before God. It was Nimrod who conceived the world's first skyscraper, known as the Tower of Babel. Daniel and Isaiah, in Daniel 2:37–39 and Isaiah 60:3, 16, give a description of one of the world's greatest Hamitic rulers, whose power was passed on to the Caucasians or Gentiles. The book of Luke, 21:24, gives an account of the Caucasians maintaining rule until Jesus Ham-Ashiah's second coming. There are other passages indicating the Black man's ancient rule.

Brother Tidwell: Dr. Johnson, were the ancient Babylonians Hamitic or Semitic? I've noticed in several Bible dictionaries that the Babylonians are called Semitic.

Dr. Johnson: The earliest Babylonians were Hamites, who are presently portrayed by the Western clergy as Semites; a maneuver used to eliminate the awareness of a biblical African presence. It is critical to understand that the Hamites and Semites were a blend of one race. The Greek Herodotus said that the only difference between the African and Eastern Ethiopians was their hair. Now, the Eastern Ethiopians are merely what we call in today's Sunday schools, "Babylonians" and "Assyrians." The Black Assyrians received their name from the word, "Ashur," meaning black.125

Sister Payne: Dr. Johnson, are Blacks Gentiles?

Dr. Johnson: Blacks are called Gentiles by the Western clergy.

However, when Genesis 10:1–6 gives a description of Noah's three sons Ham, Shem, and Japheth, only Japheth is described as a Gentile, since geographically he was destined to live in Europe, separating himself from Ham and Shem. This offered him little if any biblical participation, or any genetic link to the Messianic tree.

The term *Gentile* is mentioned 130 times in the *King James Version,* but is never linked to Ham or his children. It was after the recordance of the Old and New Testaments that Europe chose to reclassify Negroes as Gentiles. The revised bibles have frequently discarded the word Gentile in Genesis 10:5, in order to conceal this truth. Still, some Black ministers, who proclaim to be the defenders of truth, sit back saying, "what difference does it make?"

Dr. Laney: Dr. Johnson, wasn't there a group of Canaanites living in Harosheth whom the Bible referred to as Gentiles?

Dr. Johnson: Not really. The occupants of Harosheth were a foreign sea people led by Sisera to assist the indigenous Canaanites against the intrusion of Israel. The name Sisera is neither Hamitic nor Semitic.126

Mrs. Richardson: Dr. Johnson, tell us something positive about the new revised bibles.

Dr. Johnson: The new revised bibles have surely secured the word of God toward attaining salvation. But on the other hand, they have kept people of color from perceiving a biblical physical identity by distorting key Scriptures that projected a Negro presence!

To prove this claim, read Job 30:30; Song of Solomon 1:5–6; Daniel 7:9, and Revelation 1:14–15. Compare these verses with the new revised bibles. The new revised bibles have fulfilled an old conspiracy that dates back to the Nicene Council, held in 325 A.D. The objective of this council was to eliminate profound Scriptures relating to the Negro presence. This information is not difficult to understand by those who study and have the power of the Holy Spirit!

Pastor Edwards: I've always believed the Bible to be infallible. What are you saying?

Dr. Johnson: Sir, in anything that man has had his hands in, you can be assured of finding some fault.

Pastor Edwards: Doesn't II Timothy 3:16 say the Bible was written by inspired men of God?

Dr. Johnson: Yes, but remember, the translators, following those inspired men, were not always people of the same quality. For example, why do we have various translations that are different? For instance, the "Jewish Bible" has 24 books, the "King James Version" 66, the "Catholic" 73, and the "Ethiopian" 81. Again, why the difference in book quantity?

Dr. Edwards: But this has nothing to with the Bible's objective to save souls.

Dr. Johnson: You're correct, and no one in this audience has said otherwise. All I'm emphasizing is that there are many versions of the Bible that differ from the original.

Reverend Pierce: Can you furnish the audience some biblical proof of your claim?

Dr. Johnson: Well, aside from the contortion of Job 30:30; Solomon 1:5–6; Daniel 7:9 and 10:6, and Revelation 1:14–15, there are other inconsistencies in translation. In the "King James Version," before the new publication of 1979, compare II Kings 24:8 with Chronicles 36:9 which contradicts Jehoiachin's age; was he 18 or 8? Compare II Kings 8:26 with II Chronicles 22:2; was Ahaziah 22 or 42? What about I Kings 4:26 in comparison with II Chronicles 9:25? Did Solomon have 40,000 stalls of horses for his chariots and 12,000 horsemen, or 4,000 stalls of horses and 12,000 horsemen? Let's not overlook I Samuel 31:4–6 compared with II Samuel 1:1-10. Did Saul murder himself or did an Amalekite kill him? Last, but not least, observe II Samuel 10:18 in comparison to I Chronicles 19:18. Did David kill 700 charioteers and 40,000 horsemen of the Asyrians, or 7,000 charioteers and 40,000 foot soldiers of the Asyrians? Was it horsemen or foot soldiers?

Mrs. Jackson: Dr. Johnson, if you're saying that the Bible has contradictions, then you're mad!

Dr. Johnson: Most saints who promote truth are called mad. In Acts 26:24, Paul is called mad. To deny the truth is worse than being labeled mad, since it is our last hope and leg to stand on!

Dr. Williams: Dr. Johnson, comment on the various race titles we apply to our people; Negro, Colored, Black, and Afro-American.

Dr. Johnson: Some of our greatest American achievements came from a generation who used the names Colored and Negro from the time of slavery until the 1960s. They used titles that much of today's population shun, yet they would risk their lives for the cause of freedom under any circumstance. In the 1970s the new use of the term "Black" suceeded in carrying the struggle even further. However, the new generation of "Afro-Americans," appears to have abandoned this cause. They have replaced it with sports and comedy which accomplish very little compared with the martyr who once called himself Colored or Negro!

Dr. Williams, I personally believe that it's not the name that makes a people but the people behind the name.

Mrs. Pinkham: Dr. Johnson, do you have some resentment toward athletics and comedians?

Dr. Johnson: Let us use the very common sense God gave us by influencing our children to focus more on the field of scholastics. We need the best doctors and educators of the century, not the best athletes or comedians! Let's influence our children to apply their greatest potential toward their mental capacities, rather than their legs, backs, and arms. Let's seek other directions for our utopia, since we have more then our share of sportsmen and comedians. We need more scientists, historians, lawyers, and politicians.

Now, if the new generation, who prefers to be called Afro-Americans, doesn't alter its course of thinking, we will surely have another 100 years to go. Let's realize that great civilizations are not built by athletes, but by academicians; not by muscles, but by minds. The brutal strength of a bull rarely overpowers the strategy of a matador.

Mrs. Pinkham, if we think the athlete is the solution to our problem, then our future is hopeless. The physical strength of our people has been Westernly praised from slavery to modern sports. I believe it's time that Blacks demonstrate to the world that their intellectual abilities are several times greater. We need to stop putting our best talent in the wrong places!

Mr. Coolidge: Dr. Johnson, it appears that some White Americans are finally resolving their hard feelings toward people of color. What are your comments?

Dr. Johnson: Oh well, thank God for that. But could this be another form of manipulation? Let us not ignore the fact that modern day Afro-Americans are merely a dependent race under the rule of the Caucasian race. Blacks remain satisfied with the crumbs they capture from the rich man's table. Instead of devouring the heart of the pie, the Black man seeks and eats only the crust! The Afro-American still has mixed emotions concerning Africa, himself, his past, and future. When you can find a people who will sacrifice so much for so little, then why not befriend them? The freedom fighters who called themselves Blacks or Negroes cherished cohesion, and would endure public beatings, being thrown in jails, and even being killed for justice. The new generation, who prefers the title Afro-American, will witness their own brothers being dragged down the streets, and will say nothing because of their fear of losing their crumbs.

They appear to know very little about the people who died for their future. Many will take advantage of minority programs (which were previously fought for by those called Negroes, Coloreds, or Blacks), then bootlick themselves to a high social position; ultimately helping adversary groups to eliminate the very programs they used to better their lives.

Brother Hightower: Dr. Johnson I've observed how well you've verified your comments with numerous references about Ham, Cush, Egypt, and Phut being Blacks or Negroes. But what about Canaan? What sources verify him being Black, other than being a son of Ham?

Dr. Johnson: The Bible's genealogical account should be the nailing evidence. However, there are other sources such as *The Oxford English Dictionary* with 20 Volumes, which says: "How graceless Ham laughed at his Dad, which made Canaan a Nigger!" Marilyn Hickey links the Black Canaanites to the Negro race, by saying that only the Canaanites, of the whole Black race, were cursed. Professor Diop called the Canaanites "Negroes." It was during the Renaissance that Canaan, Phut, Mizraim, Cush, and Ham, were reclassified as Caucasians.127

Brother Hightower: Now that's heavy because *The Oxford English Dictionary* is internationally used. Dr. Johnson, where in the text would I find this information?

Dr. Johnson: Under the word Nigger.

Mr. Todd: Dr. Johnson, define a myth.

Dr. Johnson: A belief not based on fact or reality. The belief that Jesus possessed European features is a perfect example of a myth; it is contrary to Daniel's and John's description. Black's misunderstanding of their Biblical heritage is replaced by myth!

Mr. Todd: Dr. Johnson, can you give the audience a brief personal description of your purpose on earth?

Dr. Johnson: Sir, my purpose on earth is to serve my Creator and mankind by seeking salvation and fighting evil, which justifies my existence. May the audience be reminded that evil only strives when good men do nothing.

Mr. Todd: Dr. Johnson, I've noticed you capitalize the word God when applying to a deity other than Israel's. Why?

Dr. Johnson: That shouldn't raise any anxiety, since in Mark 13:22, the term Christ in the phrase "false Christs" is capitalized.

Mrs. Richardson: Dr. Johnson, you said that Ham was also called Or which was translated "Air." Were there other translations of Or?

Dr. Johnson: Quite a few; such as the popular term, "Ur," which was the birth place of Abraham. This information is not difficult to understand by those who acknowledge the letters *"O"* and *"U"* as interchangeable. The Deity Ham was also called El and Ham-Ur.128

Brother Hightower: Dr. Johnson, what other sources define Ham, Cush, and Phut as Negroes or Black people?

Dr. Johnson: There are several, but I'll only name a few. However, following this program I'll give you other sources. Young's *Analytical Concordance to the Bible* identifies Ham, the youngest son of Noah, (the father of Canaan), as being swarthy, dark colored. The Concordance went on to say, that the name "Egypt," the same as Kem, is equivalent to Ham, meaning Black and warm. The "Sanhedren" of *The Babylonian Talmud*, speaks of Cush as a Negro.129

Brother Hightower: Dr. Johnson, some historians state that Ham had nothing to do with the Negro. What are your comments?

Dr. Johnson: This is another form of exploitation because the name Ham means Black or Negro, according to the ancient Hebrew, Egyptian, Ethiopian, Greek, Roman, and British writers. As stated earlier, only recently have modern historians chose to slyly disassociate Ham with Blacks or Negroes.

Brother Hightower: What's your reason for the disassociation?

Dr. Johnson: To mislead the world in comprehending that Ham and his four Black sons, were the founding fathers of Philosophy and mathematical sciences; a contribution that lead to the ultra-structure of modern civilization!

Dr. Laney: Dr. Johnson, as a Christian people, name one of our greatest achievements as well as one of our greatest blunders.

Dr. Johnson: As a God-fearing people one of our greatest achievements is our demonstrated ability to forgive and love our enemies, as Jesus Ham-Ashiah, or Messiah has demanded of us. I believe our greatest blunder is our allowing Caucasians to take the sacred word Nigger or Niger, which anciently meant God, King, and Supreme, and use it as a weapon against us.

Tim: Dr. Johnson, could your comment on the four types of blood and their origins?

Dr. Johnson: Let me first say that Acts 17:26 says, "For by one blood was all nations formed." Type O blood is the master type, originating in Africa by meat eaters. As man migrated from Africa to Asia and Europe for larger game, and took up farming, they brought about A, B, and AB blood: a gradual evolution that was initiated by dieting, changing climates, and intermingling.

Dr. Peter J. D'Adamo in his book called *"Eat Right 4 Your Type."* Clearly outlined that the African type O blood, constituted the African as the father of mankind.

Sister Payne: Where do you think Blacks are headed during this Millenium?

Dr. Johnson: To a greater height, an achievement which can only be accomplished through faith and hard work. We must wake up by seeking salvation through wisdom and knowledge!130

Sister Ford: As a people, after learning of Blacks in the Bible where should we go from there?

Dr. Johnson: Through prayer and meditation we should pass this information on to our children. That way, it will not be said during this millennium, that people of color have no heritage in the Bible.

Dr. Carey: Dr. Johnson, we have held this symposium for a wonderful three hours and will cease to take any more questions from the audience since you are due at the airport in the next hour.
We will respectfully allow you have the final comment before bringing this most wonderful gathering to a close. Dr. Johnson give us your final comments.

Dr. Johnson: I thank the audience for allowing me to share these special moments in their midst. I hope that in the future we'll continue to promote knowledge and ever grow in grace. We must realize that studying the past divines the future, and that in order to unlock our future, we must first find the key to our past. We must acknowledge that it is critical that we understand from whence we came, so that our children may know where they're going. To believe our Caucasian brothers' version of a Bible that denies Black people a biblical heritage, is like believing the sky has no clouds and the forest no trees. To tell our children that their presence in the Bible is not important is sending a strong message that they're not important. Therefore, as we continue to read our Bibles, let us be aware that many of the characters therein are people of our ancestry from whom we can learn more if we seek, knock, and ask. Thank you.

Dr. Carey: Dr. Johnson, as a result of this symposium, I must sincerely say that the audience and I will be a whole lot smarter departing than before entering. Your invitation in honor of our Lord Jesus Christ has definitely uplifted our spirits and self-esteem. You have enhanced our belief that the worth of a people is determined by how they honor God, the Bible, and their heroes. We certainly appreciate your knowledge and honesty, and hope you'll continue to fufill God's plan of Salvation. We thank you Dr. Johnson, and hope that your greatest works are ahead of you.

Following this section, Dr. Johnson immediately engaged with the audience, offering additional information before his departure. Dr. Carey then assisted him to his vehicle while discussing the possibilty of a second return. Both men, with a smile and handshake, said farewell, agreeing that Dr. Johnson would return as the group's guest speaker.

INDEX OF PARTICIPANTS

Benson, 11-12, 21-22, 109-110

Carey, 2-3, 25, 59, 72, 95, 107-108, 122

Coolidge, 3-4, 7, 19-20, 32, 48-50, 56, 69, 106, 108, 117

Dupree, 14, 18, 51-55, 61, 65, 81, 89, 104, 112

Edwards, 6-7, 35, 90, 93, 100-101, 105, 110-111, 115

Ford, 15, 19, 56-57, 84, 121

Franklin, 4, 29, 43, 51, 58-59, 64-65, 71, 76-77, 93

Gibbes, 17, 37, 39, 44, 48, 53, 56, 58, 70-71, 77, 105, 107-108

Higgins, 13, 86, 90

Hightower, 31, 37, 54, 59, 79, 96, 118-120

Jackson, 8-12, 20-21, 23-24, 33, 41-43, 45, 54, 57, 66, 81, 116

Jason, 73, 75, 95, 99, 101, 111

Jefferson, 20, 40, 110

Jones, 8-9, 16, 18, 30-31, 40, 78, 80, 87, 100

Laney, 66, 68, 71, 79, 84, 90, 106, 114, 121

Lott, 23, 38, 58, 67, 70, 102-103

Louis, 15, 41, 49, 53, 111

Melissa, 60-61, 85, 90, 98-99, 111

Payne, 32, 46, 57, 62, 80, 113, 121

Petterson, 25, 28

Pierce, 28-29, 43-44, 57, 62, 85, 115

Pinkham, 13, 15-16, 21, 24, 30, 34-36, 38, 45, 47-48, 55, 112, 117

Richardson, 6, 15, 18, 33-35, 37, 40-41, 51, 63, 65, 97, 110, 114, 119

Tidwell, 9, 12, 36, 54, 63-64, 92, 113

Tim, 76, 89, 98, 112, 121

Todd, 45, 47, 55-56, 66-67, 88, 92, 119

Williams, 116

REFERENCES

1. Philo Supplement I, *Questions and Answers on Genesis*, pp. 7-8; Rudolph Windsor, *From Babylon to Timbuktu*, p. 14. 1986; and *The Life and Works of Flavius Josephus* (The Gihon was the Nile in Africa), Whiston, p. 33.

2. *The King James Version* (not the new, published in 1979), Gen. 14:5; I Chron. 4: 40; 21:16; Hab. 3:7; Es. 1:1; 8:9 *His Pilgrimage* (The Negro King Ganges marched his Ethiopian army deep into Asia and subdued territories as far as the River Ganges, to which he left his name, being previously called Chliaros) Purchas, p. 511. 1905–1907; *History of Mankind* (A Negritic people inhabited Asia), Ratzell, p. 547; *A New History of India* (Cush invaded India and founded dynasties for more than a century), Wolpert, p. 13. 1982; and *Life of Apollonius* (The Ethiopians were an Indian race), Philostratus, Book 3, (xx) 271.

3. *Ethiopia and The Missing Link in African History* (Hindu Cush), Means, pp. 38, 70. 1990.

4. *The King James Version* (not the new, published in 1979), Gen. 2:10; Isa. 29:8; 55:1; John 3:5; 4:10, 14; Rev. 22:1; *The Macmillan Bible Atlas* (Pishon is the Blue Nile), Aharoni and Avi-Yonah, p. 21. 1977; *The Life and Works of Flavius Josephus* (The Gihon was the Nile in Africa), Whiston, p. 33; *Ethiopia and The Missing Link in African History,* Means, (Josephus says the Greeks called the Nile the River of Ham), p. 12. 1990; *The New Encyclopedia Britannica Dictionary,* 15th. ed. Vol. 22, p. 602. 1991; *The Oxford Hindi-English Dictionary* (Yam means Night), McGregor, p. 843, 1993; *A Comprehensive Persian-English Dictionary* (Rain means Hama or Ham; Yam means Ham), Steingass, pp. 409, 1507, 1527. 1975; *Ugaritic Manual* (Yamm means God and sea), Gordon, pp. 47, 55. 1955; *New*

International Dictionary of Old Testament Theology and Exegesis (Yam means God), W.A. VanGemeren, Vol. 5, p. 756. 1997; *A Complete Hebrew-English Pocket-Dictionary to the Old Testament* (Yam means Euphrates, sea lake, large rivers), Feyerabend, p. 127. 1931; *The Zohar* (Yam means Sea; Hym (Him or Ham) means water), I Copy, Vol. 1, pp. 75, 115, Soncino Press, 1933; *A Dictionary of Urdu Classical Hindi and English* (Yam means ocean and sea), pp. 1251-1252. 1968; *The Kabbalah Unveiled* (Hamim means water), Mathers, p. 49. 1974; Herodotus (The Greeks called the Nile Melas, meaning Niger or Black), Beloe, Vol. 1, pp. 304-305. 1821; *The Oxford English Dictionary* (see I, Ch, C, K and Cham), 20 Vox., 1989; *Material For a Sumerian Lexicon* (C equal I), Prince, p.x. 1908; *An Introduction to the Comparative Grammar of the Semitic Languages* (H equal K), Moscati, pp. 38-39, 52. 1964; and *Sanskrit-English Dictionary* (ocean and water means Kam), p. 250. 1964.

5. *Diodorus Siculus* (The Ethiopian, as historians relate, were the first of all men), Book 3; *A New System*, Bryant, Vol. 3, p. 185. 1807; *Natural Knows No Color-Line,* Rogers, p. 32. 1952; and *Wonderful Ethiopians of the Ancient Cushite Empire* (Stephanus), Houston, p. 17. 1985.

6. *Diororus Siculus* (Egypt under the Sea), Book 3; *Wonderful Ethiopians of the Ancient Cushite Empire,* Houston, p. 66. 1988; *Great African Thinkers* (Egypt under the sea), Ivan Van Sertima, p. 44. 1992; and *Unger's Bible Dictionary* (Pliny), p. 328. 1957.

7. *The African Origin of Civilization,* Diop, p. 281. 1974; *Ethiopia and The Missing Link in Africa History* (Negritic China), Means, pp. 73-75. 1990; *The Lincoln Library* (Negritos means little Negroes), p. 520. 1971; *American Anthropologist,* Vol. 7, p. 29. 1909; Les Negritoes; and *A Compartive Grammar of the Semitic Languages* (M = N), O'Leary, 1923: 64, 77, 106.

8. See Encyclopedia.

9. *The Life of Apollonius*, p. 57; Anacalypsis, Higgins, pp. 357, 536. 1836; *Zenith of Egyptian Power,* Breasted, in 37, Vol. 11, p. 88; *The Ancient History of the Near East*, Hall, p. 231. 1920; *The Mystic Bible* (Tigris means black), Stone, p. 114. 1956; and *The Geography of Strabo*, Book, 6, p. 93; 16, p. 245.

10. *The King James Version* (not the new, published in 1979), Isa. 28:10; Acts 1:8; I Tim. 4:13; II Tim. 2:15; I Pet. 3:15; and *Sex and Race,* Rogers, Vol. 1, p. 28, 1968.

11. *The King James Version* (not the new, published in 1979), Gen. 1:29; 2:11-12; 3:1- 6.

12. *The King James Version* (not the new, published in 1979), Dan. 7:9; 10:6; Rev. 1: 14-15; 4:3, I Cor. 15:47-49; *What Color was Jesus?*, Mosley, 1987; *St. Louis Review,* Vol. 51, No. 6, February 7. 1992; *Encyclopedia Biblica* (The sardine or Sardius stone is very fine dark-red), *Black and Cheyne*, Vol. 4. p. 4287. 1903; and Newsweek, January 11, 1988.

13. *The King James Version* (not the new, published in 1979), Ho. 2:16; *Anacalypsis*, Higgins (Jescua Ham-Massiah or Jesus Homi-Num Salvator), Vol. 1, pp. 315-316, 328, 673, 780. 1836; *The Dead Sea Scroll and The Bible* (Jeshuah Ham-Mashiach), Pfeiffer, p. 126. 1969; *The Two Babylons* (Iusus Homi-Num), p. 164. 1959; *The Negro is a Man,* Armistead, pp. xvii, xxi, 89, 153, 1903; *Encyclopedia Judaica* (Messiah means Hamashiah), Vol. 11, p. 1407. 1971; *The Jewish Encyclopedia* (Messiah means Hamashiah), Vol. 8, p. 505. 1912; *Encyclopedia Judaica* (Ha-Ra-Ham-An and Hama-Kom, see index), 1972; *The Universal Jewish Encyclopedia* (Hama-Kom and El Rahum, see God), Vol. 5, p. 191. 1969; *Hebrew and Babylonian Traditions* (The terms Baal and Yahweh were almost interchangeable), Jastrow, p. 29.

1941; and *Encyclopedia Judaica* (see God, Names of), Vol. 7. 1971.

14. *Egypt's Place* (Kam [Ham] means copper and bronze), Bunsen, Book 1, p. 588. 1854; *Books on Egypt and Chaldaea,* Budge, Vol. 31, p. 262. 1911; *Universal Jewish Encyclopedia* (Kam means Ham), Vol. 4, p. 5. 1941; *A Practice Sanskrit Dictionary* (Kam-Sa means brass), p. 60. 1954; *Webster's Third New International Dictionary* (see black copper), 1971; *The Universal Jewish Encyclopedia* (Kam means Ham), Vol. 4, p. 5. 1941; *An Egyptian Hieroglyphic Dictionary* (Hemt [Ham] means copper. Hemt-Kam means black copper), Budge, pp. 485-86, 1978; *The Anchor Bible Dictionary* (Ham means Hmt (Hemt), Vol. 3, p. 32, 1992; and *Echoes of the Old Darkland* (Ham, Cham or Kam means Black), Finch, p. 133. 1991.

15. *The King James Version* (not the new, published in 1979), Gen. 16:1-3; 34:21; 38: 2-3; Judg. 3:5-6; I King 11:1-2; Ezra 9: 1-2, 10, 14, 16-19, 44; Neh. 13:23; Isa. 28:10; Ezek. 16:1-3; Amos 9:7; Zeph. 3: 10; Acts 1:8; I Tim. 4:13; II Tim. 2:15; I Pet. 3:15; *Nature Knows No Color-Line,* Rogers, p. 123. 1952; *The Pale Fox, Griaule and Dieterien,* translated by S.C. Stephen, Chino Valley: *Continuum Foundation,* p. 157. 1986; *Echoes of the Old Darkland,* Finch, pp. 141, 173. 1991; *American Anthropolologist,* Vol. 5, p. 89, and *The Jew,* pp. 117, 120-134, 146-149, 174, 178, 181; and *The Lost Tribe: A Myth* (see maps of the Hebrew dispersal throughout Africa), Godbey, 1930; *The Lost Tribes: A Myth* (see map), Godbey, 1930; and Hebrew Man (Hebrews possessed flat and pug noses), Kohler, pp. 16, 24, 1956.

16. *The King James Version* (not the new, published in 1979), Dan. 7:9; 10:6; Rev. 1: 14-15; 2:18.

17. *Encyclopedia of Religion and Ethics* (Adam was called Ad-

Ham), Vol. 1, p. 84. 1908; Jones' Dictionary of Old Testament Proper Names (Ad-Ham also mean "Lord Ham"), p. 91. 1990; *A Comprehensive Persian-English Dictionary* (Adham means Black), Steingass, p. 30, 1975; *A New System* (Adam and Ham were called Adham and Lord Ham), Bryant, Vol. 1, pp. 30, 69; Vol. 4, p. 267. 1807; *Dr. William Smith's Dictionary of the Bible*, Vol. 4, 3648. 1890; *Sacred Books and Early Literature of the East*, Horne, Vol. 1, p. 226. 1917; *Egyptian Language* (Am means Hebrew English Lexicon (Adam was reddish brown): *The Hebrew and Chaldee Words in the Old Testament Scriptures with their Meaning in English*, p. 4, Bagster & Sons; *Assyrian Dictionary* (dark red earth), pt. 1, p. 95. 1964; *The Beginning of History* (Adamu means Black), Lenormant, pp. 310-314. 1899; *Encyclopedia Judaica* (see Adam), Vol. 1. 1971; and *The Oxford English Dictionary* (see Ud; Ham means Am), 20 Vols., 1989.

18. December 20th issue of *Jet*, by Johnson Publication, p. 23. 1982; and *Les Blancs d'Afrique*, Weisgerber, p. 83. 1910.

19. *The King James Version* (not the new, published 1979), Gen. 1:5; *Unger's Bible Dictionary*, p. 293. 1957; *Encyclopedia Judaica* (Ha-Ra-Ham-An and Hama-Kom, see index), 1972; *The Oxford Latin Dictionary*, p. 785. 1982; *Strong's Exhaustive Concordance: Greek Dictionary* (ainigma): No. 135; *Encyclopedia Biblica* (see sardius), Cheyne, Vol. 4, p. 4287. 1903; *The Universal Jewish Encyclopedia* (Hama-Kom and El Rahum, see God), Vol. 5, p. 191. 1969; *Dr. William Smith's Dictionary of the Bible* (God was called "Shem Hamme-Phor-Ash"), Vol. 2, p. 1238. 1890; *The Madrash on Psalms* (Shem Hame-For-Ash), Graude, Vol. 2, 1961; *The New International Dictionary of Old Testament Theology and Exegesis* (The Semites worshiped the Sun God Hammu), VanGemeren, Vol. 2, pp. 172, 177, 614. 1997; *The Negro is a Man* (Ham means Black), pp. xii-xix, xx, xxii, 8, 102- 103, 105, 128-129, 531. 1901; *Jones' Dictionary of Old Testament Proper Names* (Ham

means Black and Niger), Jones, p. 138. 1990; *A Comparative Grammar of the Semitic Languages* (K = Kh, H, G and S), O'Leary, pp. 52, 61-62. 1923; *An Introduction to the Comparative Grammar of The Semitic Languages* (K = S, H, Q and G), Moscati, pp. 38-39. 1964; *The Oxford English Dictionary* (Ham means Hama), 20 Vols., 1989; *The Zohar* (God is called Has-Hamma-Im and Mah), I Copy, Vol. 1, pp. 5-8, 15, 65, Soncino Press. 1933; and *Encyclopedia Judaica* (see God, Names of), Vol 7, 1971.

20. *Roget's 21st Century Thesaurus*, Kipler, p. 112, 1992.

21. December 20th issue of *Jet*, by Johnson Publication, p. 23, 1982.

22. Pliny Ep. vi. p. 28; *The Macmillan Bible Atlas* (Havilah, Aharoni and Avi-Yonah, p. 21. 1977; *The Original African Heritage Study Bible,* pp. Ix, xi. 1993; and *The Valley of the Dry Bones* (Havilah), Rudolph Windsor, p. 132. 1986.

23. U.S. News, September 16, 1991; *The Mediterranean Races*, Sergi, 1901; *Race Prejudice*, Jean Finot, p. 99; *The Origin of the Aryan*, Taylor, p. 96; *The Influence of the Geographic Environments*, Churchill, p. 121; *Great African Thinkers* (The origin of man), Ivan Sertima, Vol. 1, 1986; and *Inter-Racial Problems*, Sir Harry H. Johnston.

24. *The Mediterranean Races*, Sergi, 1901.

25. *History of Ancient Civilization*, C. Seignobos; *The Jewish Encyclopedia* (Messiah means Hamashiah), Vol. 8, p. 505. 1912; *The Seven Great Monarchies*, Rawlinson, Vol. 1; *Ancient History*, C. Rollin (Zeus was Ham), Vol. 3, pp. 217-218, 1661-1741; *A New System*, Bryant (Zeus was Ham; Cush was Apollo), Vol. 1, pp. 5-6, 81; Vol. 2, pp. 52-53. 1807; and *The Two*

Babylons, Hislop, p. 49. 1959; *World's Great Men of Color* (Sheba), Rogers, Vol. 1, p. 87. 1972; *Nature Knows No Color-Line* (Negroes are deified), Rogers, p. 31. 1951; *A Comprehensive Persian English Dictionary* (Ham means Master), Steingass, p. 1508. 1975; *Elementary Egyptian Grammar* (Hem means Majesty), Murray, p. 104. 1932; *Encyclopedia of Religion and Ethics* (Elo means God), Hastings, Vol. 9, pp. 401-403. 1917; *Hebrew and Babylonian Traditions* (The terms Baal and Yahweh were almost interchangeable), Jastrow, p. 29. 1941; *The History of Herodotus,* Rawlingson, p. 108, 1941; *Jamieson, Fausset and Brown Commentary on the Whole Bible* (Ham means Amon, No, Ammon and No-Ammon), p. 650, 1961; and *Funk & Wagnalls Standard Family Dictionary* (Amen means Jesus, Ammon, Amon, Amon-Re, Amen-Ra or Egypt's Sun-God), Vol. 1, p. 39, 1961. *Bible Defence of Slavery,* Josiah Priest, pp. 54, 68, 69, and 283.

26. *The King James Version* (not the new, published in 1979), Judg. 1:21; 3:5-6; Ezra 9:1-2; 10:14, 16-19; Ps. 87: 1-7; Isa. 28:10; Ezek. 16:1-3; Dan. 7:9; 10:6; Amos 9:7; Zeph. 3:10; Acts 1:8; I Tim. 4:13; II Tim. 2:15; I Pet. 3:15; Rev. 1:14-15; Book 5, Chap. 2, Tacitus; *American Anthropologist* (Fishberg), Vol. 5, p. 89. 1903; *The Jew* (Negro Jews), pp. 117, 120-134, 146-149, 174, 178, 181; *The Egyptian Book of the Dead* (The Egyptian religion was converted into Christianity), Massey, pp. 13, 91. 1994; *Echoes of the Old Darkland* (Jews described as Negroes), Finch, pp. 141, 173. 1991; *Religions of the World* (The Babylonian beliefs are combined into the Old Testament), Berry, p. 13. 1968; *The Babylonian Genesis,* Heidel Alexander, 1963; *Proof of the Accuracy of the Bible* (see Code of Hammurabi and the Mosaic law), David Village, 1973; *The Lost Tribe: A Myth* (see map concerning the Hebrew dispersal of Africa), Godbey, 1930; and *Anacalypsis* (Christianity is not new), Higgins, Vol. 2, p. 42. 1886.

27. *The King James Version* (not the new, published in 1979), Gen. 10:1, 6, 9-10; 11:26, 28; 12:1-3; Josh. 24:2; Ps. 87: 4; Isa. 19:21-22, 25; 43:3-4; Dan. 3:25; Matt. 20:28; Mark 10:45; I Tim. 2:6; Heb. 9:15; *The Midrash on Psalms* (Jesus was This Man and That Man), Braude, Vol. 13, p. 77. 1959; and *Diodorus* (The Egyptians learned the greater part of their laws from the Ethiopians. The Egyptian borrowed the writing hieroglyphic from the Ethiopians), Book 3.

28. *A New System* (Ham means I Am-Us), Bryant, Vol. 1, pp. 320-321. 1807; *The Oxford English Dictionary* (see Cham, Ch and I), 20 Vols., 1989; and *Strong's Exhaustive Concordance* (I Am and Am): 1961.

29. *Hebrew Union College Annual*, Lewy, Vol. 18, pp. 473-480. 1944; Vol. 23, p. 373. 1950 & 1951; *Studies in Hebrew Proper Names,* G.B. Gray, pp. 44, 52. 1896; *The Origin of Races and Color* (Ham was Jupiter), Delany, pp. 37, 42, 49, 57-58, 61. 1879; *Sacred Books and Early Literature of the East* (Am or Amma was the Old Testament Ham), Horne, Vol. 1, p. 226. 1917; Dr. *William Smith's Dictionary of the Bible* (Am means Ham and Ammon), Vol. 4, p. 3648, 1890; *Hebrew and Babylonian Traditions* (The terms Baal and Yahweh were almost interchangeable), Jastrow, p. 29, 1941; *Diodorus* (The Egyptians learned the greater part of their laws from the Ethiopians. The Egyptian borrowed the writing hieroglyphic from the Ethiopians), Book 3; and *The History of Herodotus,* Rawlinson, p. 108. 1941.

30. *The King James Version* (not the new, published in 1979), Gen. 1:2; Isa. 28:10; Acts 1:8; I Tim. 4:13; II Tim. 2:15; I Pet. 3:15.

31. Ibid. I John 1:5.

32. Ibid. Gen. 1:1-3.

33. *The King James Version* (not the new, published in 1979), Gen. 15:12-13; Ex. 19:9; 20:21; I king 8:10-12; Deut. 5:22-24; Matt. 13:11; I Cor. 4:1; Rev. 10:7; *Strong's Exhaustive Concordance:* No. 135; *The Legends of the Jews*, Vol. 2, p. 303. 1925; *Mythology Among the Hebrews and its Historical Development*, Goldziher, 1967; and *Mythology of all Races*, Vol. 12, pp. 94, 97, 413.

34. *The King James Version* (not the new, published in 1979), Gen. 15:12-13; Ex. 19:19-20; 20:21; Deut. 5:22-24; 16:1; I king 8:10-12; Ps. 18:11; 97:2; 99:7; Isa. 45:3.

35. *The King James Version* (not the new, published in 1979), Ex. 19:9; 20:21; Ps. 17:8; 18:11; 97:2; 136:12; 139:11; Isa. 45:7; and *The Origin of Races and Color* (Ham means positive, Shem; medium, and Japheth; Negative), M.R. Delany, p. 24. 1879 & 1991.

36. *The King James Version* (not the new, published in 1979), Isa. 28:10; Matt. 10:27; 13:44; 28:1; Mark 16:1-2; 28:1; Luke 23: 44-45; 24:1; John 20:1-3; Acts 1:8; I Tim. 4:13; II Tim. 2:15; I Pet. 3:15.

37. *The King James Version* (not the new, published in 1979), I John 2:9-11; Ho. 4: 6; and *The Origin of Races and Color* (Ham means positive, Shem; medium, and Japheth; Negative), M.R. Delany, p. 24. 1879 & 1991.

38. *The King James Version* (not the new, published in 1979), Gen. 1:1-3; Song of Sol. 1:5; Isa. 45:7; Rev. 1:18-19.

39. *Dr. William Smith's Dictionary of the Bible* (Ham means Am), Vol. 4, p. 3648. 1890; *Anacalypsis* (Am means Ham), Higgins, Vol. 1, pp. 111, 318, 623. 1836; *A New System*, Bryant, Vol. 1, p. 3. 1807; (Ham means Am or Ammon), Vol. 4, p. 3648, 1890;

Sacred Books and Early Literature of the East (Am or Amma was the Old Testament Ham), Horne, Vol. 1, p. 226. 1917; and *The Oxford English Dictionary* (see Im, Him and Ham), 20 Vols., 1989.

40. *The King James Version* (not the new, published in 1979), Rev. 1:18-19; 3:14; *Fausset's Bible Dictionary* (Ham means Amen, Amon, Aman and Hamon), pp. 34, 269, 513. 1961; *The Religions of Ancient Egypt and Babylonia* (Amen is represented by Haman), p. 252. 1902; *Jones' Dictionary of Old Testament Proper Names* (Hamon is linked to Ham), Jones, p. 138. 1990; *Sacred Books and Early Literature of the East* (Am or Amma was the Old Testament Ham), Horne, Vol. 1, p. 226. 1917; *Dr. William Smith's Dictionary of the Bible,* Vol. 4, p. 3648. 1890; and *The Jewish Encyclopedia* (Messiah means Hamashiah), Vol. 8, p. 505. 1912.

41. *A Comprehensive Persian English Dictionary*, F. Steingass, p. 1527. 1975.

42. *The King James Version* (not the new, published in 1979), Rev. 1:18-19; 3:14; *A Basic Grammar of the Ugaritic Language* (Hym [Him or Ham] means Life), Segert, p. 185. 1984; *Dictionary of First Names* (Hyam or Chaim means Life), Hodges, p. 160. 1990; *Webster's New World Hebrew Dictionary* (Come back to life means Kam, Resurrection and Rose), p. 163. 1992; *Jewish Family Names* (Chaim or Haim means Life), Guggenheimer, pp. 152, 315. 1992; *Universal Jewish Encyclopedia* (Kam means Ham), Vol. 4, p. 5. 1941; *Outpouring* (Ham is derived from the Egyptian name Kam), Hickey, Nov., Vol. 15, No. 11, 1992: P.O. Box 17340, Denver, Co. 80111; *Young's Analytical Concordance to the Bible* (Kem or Egypt is equivalent to Ham, meaning Black and warm. Ham also means swarthy-dark colored), p. 443. 1982; *A Comprehensive Persian-English Dictionary* (Cham means "a living creature"), F.

Steingass, p. 398. 1975; *Fausset's Bible Dictionary* (Ham means Amen, Amon, Aman and Hamon), pp. 34, 269, 513. 1961; *The Religions of Ancient Egypt and Babylonia* (Amen is represented by Haman), p. 252. 1902; *Dr. William Smith's Dictionary of the Bible* (Ham means Am), Vol. 4, p. 3648. 1890; *Anacalypsis* (Am means Ham), Higgins, Vol. 1, pp. 111, 318, 623. 1836; *A New System*, Bryant, Vol. 1, p. 3. 1807; (Ham means Am or Ammon), Vol. 4, p. 3648, 1890; *Sacred Books and Early Literature of the East* (Am or Amma was the Old Testament Ham), Horne, Vol. 1, p. 226. 1917; *The Oxford English Dictionary* (see Im, Him and Ham), 20 Vols., 1989; *A Basic Grammar of the Ugaritic Language* (Hym [Him or Ham] means Life), Segert, p. 185. 1984; *Funk & Wagnalls Standard Family Dictionary* (Amen means Jusus, Ammon, Amon, Amen-Re, Amen-Ra or Egypt's Sun-God), Vol. 1, p. 39. 1961; *Jamieson, Fausset and Brown Commentary on the Whole Bible* (Ham means Amon, No, Ammon and No-Ammon), p. 650, 1961; and *Jones' Dictionary of Old Testament Proper Names* (Hamon is linked to Ham), p. 138. 1990.

43. *The Septuagint Version.*

44. *The Ancient Hebrew Tradition*, Hommel, p. 15. 1897.

45. *The King James Version* (not the new, published in 1979), Dan. 7:9; 10:6; II Tim. 3:16; John 1:1; Heb. 1:1-2; Rev. 1:14-15; 4:3.

46. Ibid. Dan. 7:9; 10:6; I John 4:2-3; Rev. 1:14-15; 2:18; 21:8, 27; 22:15.

47. *Nature Knows No Color-Line*, Rogers, p. 123. 1952; *The Pale Fox,* Griaule and Dieterien, translated by S.C. Stephen, Chino Valley: Continuum Foundation, p. 157. 1986; and *Echoes of the Old Darkland,* Finch, p. 141. 1991.

48. *The King James Version* (not the new, published in 1979), Gen. 16:1-3; 34:21; 38: 2-3; Judg. 3:5-6; I King 11:1-2; Ezra 9: 1-2, 10, 14, 16-19, 44; Neh. 13:23; Ho. 11: 1; Ps. 68:31; Ezek. 16:1-3; Matt. 1: 1-5; 2:13-15; *From Babylon to Timbuktu,* Windsor, 1988; St. Louis Review, Vol. 51. No. 6, February 7, 1992; *What Color was Jesus?*, Mosley, 1987; *American Anthropologist* (Fishberg), Vol. 5, p. 89. 1903; *Echoes of the Old Darkland* (Jews described as Negroes), Finch, pp. 141, 173. 1991; *The Jew* (Negro Jews), pp. 117, 120-134, 146-149, 174, 178, 181.

49. *The King James Version* (not the new, published in 1979), I John 4:2-3; II Peter. 1:5.

50. Ibid. Ezek. 1:1-28; Dan. 7:9; 10:6; Rev. 1:14-15; 2:18, 4:3.

51. *The King James Version* (not the new, published in 1979), Gen. 9:18; Josh. 2:1; 6: 1; I Chron. 2:11-13; Ruth 4:21; Matt. 1: 5; *Jewish Family Names*, Guggenheimer (Sal and Zalmon mean dark skin man), pp. 652, 856. 1992; *Unger's Bible Dictionary* (See Salmon and Salma), p. 955. 1957; and *The Oxford English Dictionary* (see Solomon and Salmon), 20 Vols., 1989.

52. *The King James Version* (not the new, published in 1979), Matt. 1:5-6; Luke 3: 23, 27, 31-32; Ruth 4:13, 20-22.

53. Ibid. Isa. 33:6; Ro. 11:33; I Cor. 12:8; 13:1-2; II Peter 3:18.

54. *The King James Version* (not the new, published in 1979), I Kings 16:28, 30-31; II Kings 8: 16, 25-26; 11:1; II Chron. 22:2-3; Matt. 1:1-25; and Bible Defence of Slavery (Jezebel was a Negro), Priest, pp. 187-188. 1853.

55. *The King James Version* (not the new, published in 1979), II Tim. 1:7.

56. *Blacks in Antiquity* (Ethiopian), Snowden, 1970; *The Destruction of Black Civilization* (Black Egyptians; the word Chemi or Chem [Egypt] indicated the Black people, not the soil), Williams, pp. 68, 112, 115, 145, 163. 1976; Outpouring, Hickey, Nov., Vol. 15, No. 11, 1992: P.O. Box 17340, Denver, Co. 80111; and *The Oxford English Dictionary* (Nigger), 20 Vols., 1989.

57. *American Antiquity*, Josiah Priest, pp. 15-19. 1833.

58. *International Bible Dictionary* (Ham, the father of Cush, Mizraim, Phut, Canaan, and the Africans in general, was burnt-swarthy black), p. 182, Logos International, Plainfield, New Jersey, 1977; *Encyclopedia Judaica* (Cush or Cushi in Hebrew means Negro), Vol. 5, p. 1174. 1971; *Peloubet's Bible Dictionary* (Ham is defined as Black), Grand Rapids, Mich., Zondervan Publishing House; *Outpouring* (Ham and Cush mean Black; Phut or Libya meant Black), Hickey, Nov., Vol. 15, No. 11, 1992: P.O. Box 17340, Denver, Co. 80111; *Blacks in Antiquity* (Black Kush or Ethiopians), Snowden, 1970; *The African Origin of Civilization* (Egypt, a Negro Nation), pp. ix, xiv. 1974; and *Young's Analytical Concordance to the Bible* (Kem or Egypt is equivalent to Ham, meaning Black and warm. Ham also means swarthy-dark colored), p. 443. 1982; *The Negro is a Man* (Ham is called Black and Negro), Armistead, pp. xiii-xiv, xx, xxii, 8, 102-103, 105, 128-129, 531. 1903; *The New American Bible* (The issue concerning Ham and Canaan offers no justification for enslaving Negroes, even though Canaan was a son of Ham), p. 14. 1970; *The Message Magazine* (The origin of the Negro is traced to Ham), Vol. 40, No. 6, September, 1974, Sothern Association, Box 59, Nashville, Tennessee 37202; and *Harper's Bible Dictionary* (Ham's is believed to be the ancestor of Africans as as his brother Shem was of the Semites and Japheth of the Europeans), Miller, p. 242. 1952; *American Antiquities*, Josiah Priest, pp. 14-19. 1833; *The African Origin of Civilization*, Diop, pp. 7-8. 1974; Pedrals, op. cit., p. 27; *An Egyptian*

Hieroglyphic Dictionary, Vol. 2, p. 787. 1978; and *Echoes of the Old Darkland,* Finch, p. 133. 1991.

59. *The King James Version* (not the new, published in 1979), Matt. 10:14; I Cor. 14: 38.

60. *The King James Version* (not the new, published in 1979), Gen. 10:8-10; 11:3-9; Acts 7:22; *The Black People of American* (Culturally, the Africans were ahead of Europeans for thousands of years), Dennis, p. 7. 1970; *We Europeans* (The wheel, building in stone, agriculture and the art of writing are the fundamental discoveries on which civilization is built. The founding fathers were not of Europe), p. 94. 1935; *The History of Herodotus* (The root of Greek religion ascended from African cosmology), Herodotus, p. 99. 1928; *American Historical Review* (While Egypt was a civilized world, Europe was a land of wilderness and slavery for some two thousand years), James Henry Breasted, p. 219. 1929; *Stolen Legacy* (The Greeks learn their philosophy from the Egyptians), G.G.M. James, 1976; *Les Grand Inities* (Whites learn two essentials from Blacks, the smelting of metals and the sacred writing of hiero- glyphic), 1931; and *Philosophy of Ancient History* (The Hamites were the fountainhead of civilization), Bunsen, p. 52.

61. *The Life and Works of Flavius Josehus*, Whiston, pp. 252-253. 1957; *From Babylon to Timbuktu*, Windsor, p. 38. 1988; *American Antiquities* (Sheba was Black), Josiah Priest, pp. 35-36. 1833; *Blacks in Antiquities*, Snowden, pp. 202-203. 1970; and *Ethiopia and the Bible*, Schweich Lectures, pp. 3-4, 10, 130. 1967.

62. *The King James Version* (not the new, published in 1979), II Chron. 21:16; Hab. 3:7; and *The Family Bible*, Baird and Dillon, pp. 7-11. 1884.

63. *The International Standard Bible Encyclopedia*, Vol. 1, p. 406, 1979. *Ethiopia and the Missing Link in African History*, Means, p. 160. 1980; *The Anchor Bible Dictionary* (Cush means Kus, Cossaea, Kas, Kusi, Kas-Su and Kas-Site), p. 1219. Vol. 1. 1992; *Encyclopedia Judaica* (Cush or Cushi means Negro), p. 1174. Vol. 5. 1971; *The Lincoln Library*, Vol. 1, p. 298. 1971; *The Gods of The Egyptians* (see Par), Budge, Vol. 2, p. 19. 1969; *Egyptian Language* (Per means House), Budge, p. 151. 1966; and *The Oxford English Dictionary* (see home, Hame and Ham), 20 Vols., 1989.

64. *Washington Post* (Many of the earliest Madonnas were painted black, until the paintings of the Renaissance [Michelangelo 1475-1564] when it became popular to paint the Madonna, Mary, white, May 4, 1979; *The Black Biblical Heritage*, Johnson, p. 203. 1999; *What Color was Jesus?*, Mosley, 1987; Sepia, Dec. p. 16. 1980; and *Our Lady of the Hermits*, Raber, 1959.

65. *The King James Version* (not the new, published in 1979), Rev. 2:9; 3:9; *The One Primeval Language*, "The Fall," Forster, p. 330. 1854; *From Babylon to Timbuktu*, Windsor, 1988; *The Jewish Light* (The Ethiopian Jew), February 12, 1992, Vol. 45, No. 7; *Encyclopedia Judaica* (see Negro or Black Jews; also Cochin Jew), 1971; *Echoes of the Old Darkland* (The ancient Jews were Ethiopians and Egyptians), pp. 141, 173.

66. *The King James Version* (not the new, published in 1979), Isa. 28:10; Matt. 26:47- 48; Acts 1:8; I Tim. 4:13; II Tim. 2:15; I Pet. 3:15.

67. *The King James Version* (not the new, published in 1979), Acts 21:38-39; The Messiah Jesus (Paul's snub nose), R. Eisler, pp. 447-50. 1931; Anacalypsis, Higgins, Vol. 1, p. 801. 1836; and Original African Heritage Study Bible, Peebles, 1993; and Hebrew Man (Hebrews possessed flat and pug noses), Kohler,

pp. 16, 24, 1956.

68. *The King James Version* (not the new, published in 1979), Gen. 26:24; 28:13; 32:9; Isa. 11:1; John 8:37; Ro. 11:1; II Cor. 11:15-22; Rev. 22:16.

69. *The King James Version* (not the new published in 1979), Dan. 5:25; Rev. 3:14; *A Comparative Grammar of the Semitic Languages* (T and K equal C), O'Leary, pp. 55, 90, 242. 1923; *Egyptian Grammar* (The T equal C), Gardiner, p. 27. 1950; *On Psyeudo-Corrections in Some Semitic Languages* (T equal C), Blau, 19-20, 54. 1970; *The Jewish Encyclopedia* (Messiah means Hamashiah), Vol. 8, p. 505. 1912; *Anacalypsis*, Higgins (Jescua Ham-Massiah or Jesus Homi-Num Salvator), Vol. 1, pp. 315-316, 328, 673. 1836; *The Dead Sea Scroll and the Bible* (Jeshuah Ham-Mashiach), Pfeiffer, p. 126. 1969; *The Two Babylons* (Iusus Homi-Num), p. 164. 1959; *The Negro is a Man,* Armistead, pp. xvii, xxi, 89, 153, 1903; *Encyclopedia Judaica* (Messiah means Hamashiah), Vol. 11, p. 1407. 1971; *The Universal Jewish Encyclopedia* (Hama-Kom and El Rahum, see God), Vol. 5, p. 191. 1969; *Sex and Race* (Ni), Rogers, Vol. 1, p. 86; *Africa's Gift to America*, Rogers, p. 61. 1961; *Dictionary of the Bible* (Ni means Ne or No), Hastings, Vol. 3, p. 55. 1903; *A Commentary, Critical and Explanatory, on the Old and New Testaments* (No [Ni] means Amon [Amen], Amen-Re or Ham), Fausset, Vol. 1, pp. 551, 700. 1870; *Fausset's Bible Dictionary* (No means Amen, Amon, No, Ni'a or Ham), Fausset, pp. 34, 269, 513. 1961; *A New System* (Ham means Amon), Bryant, Vol. 1, p. 3. 1807; *The Oxford English Dictionary* (Hamy-Ne means Amen), 20 Vols., 1989; *The Negro is a Man* (Ham means Black; he was a Negro), Armistead, pp. xiii-xiv, xx, xxii, 8, 102-103, 105, 128-129, 531. 1903; *The Gods of the Egyptians* (The primeval Ni represent the watery abyss from which all things sprang), Budge, Vol. 1, p. 291; Vol. 2, p. 1. 1969; *Bible Defence of Slavery* (Ham means Black), Josiah Priest, 1853; *American Antiquities* (Ham means

Black), Josiah Priest, pp. 16, 19. 1833; *A Dictionary of the Bible* (Ham means Black), Hastings, Vol. 2, p. 288. 1911; *Jones' Dictionary of Old Testament Proper Names* (Ham means Niger or Black), p. 138. 1990; *Dr. William Smith's Dictionary of the Bible* (Ham means Black), Vol. 2, p. 984. 1889; *Dictionary of American Regional English* (Niger means Negro or Black), Cassidy, Vol. 3, pp. 788-809. 1985; *Galla-English Dictionary* (Ni means Him), Foot, p. 46. 1913; *The Ancient Hebrew Tradition* (Ni means our God), Hommel, p. 60. 1897; *Nature Knows No Color-Line* (Ger or Gir means water), J.A. Rogers, p. 72. 1952; *The Oxford English Dictionary* (God, Gad, Gar and Ger), 20 Vols., 1989; and *Africa's Gift to America*, Rogers, p. 61. 1961.

70. *Enciclopedia Universal Sopena* (Nego means Negus), Tomo Sexto, Vol. 6, p. 5947. 1964; *The Oxford English Dictionary* (Negus means King), 20 Vol., 1989; *Unger's Bible Dictionary* (Nego means God: see Abednego), p. 2. 1957; *Grande Dicionario Etimologico-Prosodico Da Lingua Portuguesa* (Nego means Negar), Vol. 6, p. 2604. 1966; *Portuguese-English Dictionary* (Nego means Negro), J.L. Taylor, p. 440, 1970; and *Concise Amharic Dictionary* (see Negus), Leslau, 1976.

71. *The King James Version* (not the new, published in 1979), Ex. 3:12; John 8:58; *The Oxford English Dictionary* (see I, Ch and C), 20 Vols., 1989; *Materials For a Sumerian Lexicon* (C = I), Prince, p. x. 1908; *The Jewish Encyclopedia* (Messiah means Ham-Ashiah), Vol. 8, p. 505. 1912; *Bible Defence of Slavery* (Ham means Black), Josiah Priest, 1853; *American Antiquities* (Ham means Black), Josiah Priest, pp. 16, 19. 1833; *A Dictionary of the Bible* (Ham means Black), Hastings, Vol. 2, p. 288. 1911; *Jones' Dictionary of Old Testament Proper Names* (Ham means Niger or Black), p. 138. 1990; *Dr. William Smith's Dictionary of the Bible* (Ham means Black), Vol. 2, p. 984. 1889; *Peloubet's Bible Dictionary* (Ham is defined as Black), Grand Papids, Mich., Zondervan Publishing House; and *Dictionary of American*

Regional English (Niger means Negro or Black), Cassidy, Vol. 3, pp. 788-809. 1985.

72. *The King James Version* (not the new, published in 1979), Isa. 28:10; Acts 1:8; I Tim. 4:13; II Tim. 2:15; I Pet. 3:15; *The Jewish Encyclopedia* (Messiah means Ham-Ashiah), Vol. 8, p. 505. 1912; *Bible Defence of Slavery* (Ham means Black), Josiah Priest, 1853; *American Antiquities* (Ham means Black), Josiah Priest, pp. 16, 19. 1833; *A Dictionary of the Bible* (Ham means Black), Hastings, Vol. 2, p. 288. 1911; *Jones' Dictionary of Old Testament Proper Names* (Ham means Niger or Black), p. 138. 1990; *Dr. William Smith's Dictionary of the Bible* (Ham means Black), Vol. 2, p. 984. 1889; *Peloubet's Bible Dictionary* (Ham is defined as Black), p. 233, Grand Papids, Mich., Zondervan Publishing House; *International Bible Dictionary* (Ham, the father of Cush, Mizraim, Phut, Canaan, and the Africans in general, was burnt-swarthy black, p. 182, Logos International, Plainfield, New Jersey, 1977; and *Dictionary of American Regional English* (Niger means Negro or Black), Cassidy, Vol. 3, pp. 788-809. 1985.

73. *The King James Version* (not the new, published in 1979), Rev. 3:14; *Dictionary of American Regional English* (Niger, Neger and Negro are synonymns), Vol. 3, p. 788, 1996; *The Oxford English Dictionary* (Negus means King), 20 Vols., 1989; *Enciclopedia Universal Sopena* (Negus means Nego), Tomo Sexto, Vol. 6, p. 5947. 1964; *Unger's Bible Dictionary* (Nego means God: see Abednego), p. 2. 1957; *Grande Dictionario Etimologico-Prosodico Da Lingua Portuguesa* (Nego means Negar), Vol. 6, 1966: 2604; *Portuguese-English Dictionary* (Nego means Negro), Taylor, p. 440. 1970; *Dr. William Smith's Dictionary of the Bible* (God's original name was changed to Shem [Sham] Hamme-Phor-Ash), Vol. 2, 1238. 1889; *Anacalypsis* (the name Om was never to be spoken), Higgins, Vol. 1, p. 233. 1836; Vol. 2, p. 170-171, 299. 1836; *Unger's Bible*

Dictionary (God was called Hu or Hue), p. 293. 1957; *Encyclopedia Judaica* (Ha-Ra-Ham-An and Hama-Kom, see index); *The Universal Jewish Encyclopedia* (Hama-Kom, see God), Vol. 5, p. 191. 1969; *Dr. William Smith's Dictionary of the Bible* (God was called "Shem Hamme-Phor-Ash"), Vol. 2, p. 1238. 1890; Bible Key Words (Hamma-Qom means God), G. Kittel, Vol. 7, p. 16. 1957; and *Jones' Dictionary of Old Testament Proper Names* (Ham was called El), pp. 296-297, 1990.

74. *A Social and Religious History of The Jews* (Yaho, a Deity in Egypt), Baron, Vol. 1, p. 352. 1952; (Yehovah)=Yahweh: The Divine Name in the Bible (Yah and Weh originated in Egypt), G. Park-Taylor, pp. 49, 71, 77. 1975; *A Dictionary Hindustani & English* (Ya was Jupiter), Forbes, p. 796. 1866; *Unger's Bible Dictionary* (Yahweh means Hu), p. 1177. 1957; and Babylonians and Assyrians (Yahum), Sayce, p. 227, 1901.

75. *The King James Version* (not the new, published in 1979), Matt. 10:22.

76. *The King James Version* (not the new, published in 1979), Ps. 87:1-7; *Diodorus Siculus* (The Ethiopian, as historians relate, were the first of all men), Book 3; *A New System*, Bryant, Vol. 3, p. 185. 1807; *Nature Knows No Color-Line,* Rogers, p. 32. 1952; *Wonderful Ethiopians of the Ancient Cushite Empire* (Stephanus), Houston, pp. 17, 197. 1985; *The Retractions*, p. 52, Catholic U Press, 1968; Oahspe Bible (Higgins), Ballou, p. 889. 1882; Black Athena, Bernal, Vol. 1, p. 23. 1987; and *A History of the Pharaohs, Weigall*, Vol. 1, p. 284. 1925.

77. *The King James Version* (not the new, published in 1979), Acts 7:22; Dan. 7:9; 10: 6; Rev. 1:14-15; 2:18; 4:3; *The Egyptian Book of the Dead* (The Egyptian religion was converted into Christianity), Massey, pp. 13, 91. 1994; *Echoes of the Old*

Darkland (Kamite religion and Christian Gospels. Chap. 5, Negative Confession), Finch, pp. 136, 198, 207. 1991; *Religions of the World* (The Babylonian beliefs are combined into the Old Testament), Berry, p. 13. 1968; *The Babylonian Genesis*, Heidel Alexander, 1963; *Proof of the Accuracy of the Bible* (see Code of Hammurabi and the Mosaic law), David Village, 1973; *Anacalypsis* (Egypt's Supreme God was black in color; Christianity is not new), Higgins, Vol. 1, pp. 134-138, Vol. 2, p. 42. 1886; and *Hebrew Union College Annual: The Old West Semitic Sun God Hammu* (Ham was worshiped by the Semites), Lewy, Vol. 18, pp. 473-480. 1944; Vol. 23, p. 373. 1950 & 1951.

78. *The World's Sixteen Crucified Saviors, or Christianity Before Christ*, Kersey Graves, 1875; The Ancient Egyptians (Ham's offspring worshiped one eternal Being and spirit, who ordained and created mankind; the Egyptians were the first to believe the soul of man is immortal), Wilkinson, Vol. 3, pp. 2, 462, 1878; and Paganism in our Christianity, Weigall, 1928.

79. *The King James Version* (not the new, published in 1979), Ps. 87:1-7; 68:31; Ho. 11:1; Matt. 2:14-15; II Pet. 1:16; The Midrash on Psalms (This man and that man refers to the Messiah), Braude, Vol. xiii, p. 76. 1959; and A History of the Pharaohs, Weigall, Vol. 1, p. 284. 1925.

80. *Encyclopedia Judaica* (see Torah); Origins, E. Partridge, p. 292. 1961; *A New System* (Osiris means Ham. The Egyptians called Law Camis), Bryant, Vol. 2, p. 328; Vol. 3, p. 81; Vol. 5 (books of Ham), pp. 200-201, 248, 290. 1807; *Jewish Family Names* (Hami-Sha, Hum-Ash and Chami-El means Pentateuch and 5), Guggenheimer, pp. 154, 319, 350. 1992; and *An Introduction of the Comparative Grammar of the Semitic Languages* (Hams means Five), Moscati, p. 116. 1964.

81. *Encyclopedia Judaica* (see Torah); Origins, E. Partridge, p. 292. 1961; *A New System* (Law means Camis), Bryant, Vol. 5, p. 248. 1807; *Jewish Family Names* (Hami-Sha, Hum-Ash and Chami-El means Pentateuch and 5), Guggenheimer, pp. 154, 319, 350. 1992; and *An Introduction of the Comparative Grammar of the Semitic Languages* (Hams means Five), Moscati, p. 116. 1964.

82. *Jewish Family Names and their Origin* (Moses), Guggenheimer, p. 529. 1992; A New System (Ham means I Am-Us), Bryant, Vol. 1, pp. 320-321. 1807; *The Oxford English Dictionary* (see Cham, Ch and I), 20 Vols., 1989; *Strong's Exhaustive Concordance: (I Am and Am):* 1961; *History of Egypt*, H. Brugsch-Bey, Vol. 2, pp. 452- 453. 1881; *The Jewish Encyclopedia* (Na means No-Amon, No and Ne), Vol. 9, p. 318. 1912; *Jones' Dictionary of Old Testament Proper Names* (No was dedicated to the Sun or Ham), Jones, pp. 279, 297. 1990; *Fausset's Bible Dictionary* (The Egyptian name of No is Amen, the sacred name of No is Ha-Amen, meaning Ham the North African God, pp. 34, 269, 513. 1961; *A Commentary, Critical and Explanatory on the Old and New Testaments* (Ham was called Amon, Ammon, No, No-Ammon, Amon the Sun and No), Rev. Fausset, Vol. 1, pp. 551, 700. 1870; *The Concise Scots Dictionary* (see Hum and Ham). 1985; *Jones' Dictionary of Old Testament Proper Names*, p. 91. 1990; *The Holy Bible According to the Authorize Version with an Explanatory and Critical Commentary, and a Revision of Translation by Bishops and Other Clergy of the Anglican Church*, F.C. Cook, (see Nahum 3:8, No of Egypt was Ham-On), F.C. Cook, Vol. 6, 1886; *Dr. William Smith's Dictionary of the Bible* (Ham means Am or Ammon), Vol. 4, p. 3648, 1890; *A Dictionary of Surnames* (Os means God; see Oswald), Hodges, p. 399. 1988; and *Sacred Books and Early Literature of the East* (Am or Amma was the Old Testament Ham), Horne, Vol. 1, p. 226. 1917; *The Dead Sea Scroll and The Bible* (Jeshuah Ham-Mashiach), Pfeiffer, p. 126.

1969; *Encyclopedia Biblica*, Cheyne, Vol. 4, p. 4287. 1903; *Encyclopedia Judaica* (Messiah means Hamashiah), Vol. 11, p. 1407. 1971; and *The Jewish Encyclopedia* (Messiah means Hamashiah), Vol. 8, p. 505. 1912.

83. *Images of Moses*, Rabbi Silver, p. 5-6. 1982; Sale (Black Moses), *Al Koran*, pp. 128, 257. 1784; *The Preaching of Islam*, p. 106, T.W. Arnold, Westminister, 1896; *The Negro is a Man*, Armistead, p. 8. 1903; and *Jewish Family Names and their Origin* (Moses), Guggenheimer, pp. 174, 526, 529. 1992.

84. *A Commentary, Critical and Explanatory, on the Old and New Testaments* (Amen means Amen-Re, Amon and Ham), Fausset, Vol. 1, pp. 551, 700. 1870; *The Oxford English Dictionary* (Hamy-Ne means Amen; Ame means Am), 20 Vols., 1989; *Dr. William Smith's Dictionary of the Bible* (Am means Ham), Vol. 4, p. 3648. 1890; *Dictionary of the Bible* (Ham is called Ames), Smith, Vol. 1, pt. 2, p. 1269, 1893; *The Jewish Encyclopedia* (Amen was later altered to Amun and Amon. The Greeks added the extra "m" = "Ammon."), Vol. 1, p. 526. 1912; *The Family Bible Dictionary* (Egypt's God Amon was called Amen the Sun), Avenel Books, p. 8. 1958; *Fausset's Bible Dictionary* (Ham means Amen, Amon, Aman and Hamon), pp. 34, 269, 513. 1961; *History of the Egyptian Religion* (Amun was called Chem), Tiele, p. 124. 1882; *The African Origin of Civilization* (Amon means Kham), Diop, p. 149. 1974; *A New System* (Ham means Amon), Bryant, Vol. 1, p. 3. 1807; Duden Fremdworterbuch Hamoglobin (see Ham), Marie Dose, 5th ed., p. 297. 1990; *Strong's Exhaustive Concordance: Greek Dictionary:* No. 129; *The World Book Dictionary* (see Hem), Thorndike Barnhart; *New International Dictionary of Old Testament Theology and Exegesis* (Ham means Bread), VanGemeren, Vol. 2, p. 177. 1997; *Gesenius's Hebrew and Chaldee Lexicon to the Old Testament Scriptures* (Ham means New Baked Bread), p. 285. 1857; *Webster's New World Hebrew*

Dictionary (Kam means Come back to life, Resurrection, and Rose), p. 163. 1992; *The Universal Jewish Encyclopedia* (Kam means Ham), Vol. 4, p. 5. 1941; *Egypt's Place* (Kam means Black and Egypt), Bunsen, Book 1, p. 615. 1854; *An Egyptian Hieroglyphic Dictionary* (Cumi [Kumi, Humi or Hami] means to rise or ascend), Budge, Vol. 1, p. 447. 1978; and *A Basic Grammar of the Ugaritic Language* (Hym [Him or Ham] means Life), Segert, p. 185. 1984.

85. *A Dictionary, Hindustani and English*, Forbes, pp. 349, 791-792. 1866; Oahspe, Ballou, p. 876. 1882; *Anacalypsis*, Higgins (Negroes first settled India; Indus represented blue-black. Herodotus called the Oriental Ethiopian Indians; the Greeks during Homer's age call the Indians Eastern Ethiopians), Vol. 1, pp. 54-55, 58-59, 357, 458, 631, 1836; *Cyclopeadia of India*, Balfour (Ind, India or Hindus means Black, Indian or Ethiopia; there were Negroes living in India), Vol. 2, pp. 56, 151, 1073-1080. 1967; Hobson-Jobson (Nigger Indians), Yule and Burnell, p. 625. 1968; *A New System*, Bryant, Vol. 4, pp. 269-278, 280. 1807; *The Century Cyclopedia of Name*, Smith (India means Ind and Indi), p. 526. 1914; *Outpouring*, Hickey (Ham, the father of Indians), Hickey, Nov., Vol. 15, No. 11, 1992: P.O. Box 17340, Denver, Co. 80111; *Calmet's Dictionary of The Holy Bible* (Hind, the son of Ham), Taylor, p. 448. 1849; *History of the Indian Tribes of the United States* (Indians are from Ham), Schoolcraft, Vol. 3, pp. 476-477. 1851; *Ethiopia and the Missing Link* (India means Ethiopia), Means, p. 71. 1980; *Cyclopaedia of Biblical Theological and Ecclesiastical Literature* (Ham's children were called Indians), Strong, Vol. 3-4, p. 36. 1969; *Black Africans and Natives Americans* (The terms Negro, Negi, Colored, and Black are used for Indians), pp. 68- 71, 73, 91, 191, 263; *Volney's New Researches Ancient History* (Ethiopia was called India; the Persians called the Ethiopians, "Hinds" and "Hindoos"), C.F. Volney, pp. 36, 175. 1856.

86. *A Dictionary of American English*, Craigie and Hulbert (Niger Heaven), Vol. 3, p. 1602. 1942; Dictionary of Word Origins, Ayto (Kamma-Ra), p. 278. 1991; Persian-English Dictionary, Steingass, pp. 643, 695-696, 758, 761, 1299, 1507. 1975; *A Dictionary of Urdu, Classical Hindi and English* (see Sama), Platts, pp. 671, 673. 1968; *A New System* (Olympus means Ham and Sham), Bryant, Vol. 1, pp. 81, 106, 296. 1807; *The Oxford English Dictionary* (see Az under the letter "I," and Khan, Han, Khan, Cham and Heven), 20 Vols., 1989; A *Comprehensive Etymological Dictionary* (Heaven means Kem or Hamma. Homo means Sama), Klein, Vol. 1, pp. 273, 712. 1966; Jewish Family Names, Guggenheimer, p. 340. 1992; *Strong's Exhaustive Concordance* (Cam means Ham and Sam): No. 5561; *The Oxford Hindi-English Dictionary* (see Car), McGregor, p. 304. 1993; *The Historical Jesus and the Mythical Christ* (Thebes means Heaven), p. 26. 1992; Origins, E. Partridge, p. 284. 1961; *A Thesaurus of Old English* (Ham means Kingdom of Heaven), Vol. 1, p. 653; Vol. 2, p. 1044. 1995; *Sanskrit-English Dictionary*, Williams, (Ri means Heaven), p. 223. 1899; *A Concise Dictionary of Old Icelandic* (Himni means Heaven), Zoego, p. 198. 1926; *The Family Bible Dictionary*, Avenel Books, p. 70. 1958; *Religions of The World* (Heaven means Kama), Berry, p. 47. 1968; *First Steps In Assyrian* (Hammanus means Quarter of Heaven), King, p. cxxxii. 1898; *Encyclopedia of Religion and Ethics*, Hastings, Vol. 2, p. 700. 1910; Vol. 6, p. 284. 1914; *The Zohar* (Heaven is Has-Hamma-Im), I Copy, Vol. 1, p. 65, Soncino Press. 1933; and *The Makers of Civilization* (Heaven means Him-In and Imin), Waddell, p. 143. 1968. 196. *The Holman Holy Bible* (see dictionary), 1891; *The Family Bible* (see dictionary), 1884; and *Bible Key Words: Basileia* (The Hebrews called God and Heaven, "Hammaqom," G. Kittel, Vol. 7, p. 16. 1957.

87. *The Oxford Hindi-English Dictionary*, McGregor, p. 1066. 1993; *Anacalypsis*, Higgins (Jescua Ham-Massiah or Jesus

Homi-Num Salvator), Vol. 1, pp. 315-316, 328, 673. 1836; *The Dead Sea Scroll and the Bible* (Jeshuah Ham-Mashiach), Pfeiffer, p. 126. 1969; *The Two Babylons* (Iusus Homi-Num), p. 164. 1959; *The Negro is a Man*, Armistead, pp. xvii, xxi, 89, 153, 1903; *Encyclopedia Judaica* (Messiah means Hamashiah), Vol. 11, p. 1407. 1971; *The Jewish Encyclopedia* (Messiah means Hamashiah), Vol. 8, p. 505. 1912; *Dictionary of American Regional English* (Nagar and Neager (Neiger) means Niger or Nigger), Vol. 3, p. 788. 1985; *Encyclopedia Judaica* (Ha-Ra-Ham-An and Hama-Kom, see index), 1972; and *The Universal Jewish Encyclopedia* (Hama-Kom and El Rahum, see God), Vol. 5, p. 191. 1969.

88. *Sanskrit Reader* (Me and Ma means Aham), Lanman, p. 210. 1963; *Oahspe Bible* (Ham is called Aham), Ballou, p. 131. 1882; *Vietnamese-English Dictionary* (Ham means Me), p. 26, 1st Psyop Bn Element, 4th Psyop Group Fort Bragg, N.C.; *The Oxford English Dictionary* (see I, Ch and Cham; Negus means King), 20 Vols., 1989; *Anacalypsis*, Higgins (Le, La, Li or Lu is God), Vol. 1, pp. 344, 428-430, 582. 1836; *Middle English Nicknames* (Le means Him), Jonsjo, 1979; *Northwest Semitic Grammar and Job* (Le and Lo is God), Blommerde, p. 28. 1969; *Collins Robert French Dictionary* (Le & Les means Homme), pp. 406, 465. 1993. *A Dictionary of Modern Written Arabic* (Ahamm, Hamma, and Humm means Black), Wehr, p. 204. 1976; *A Dictionary of the Bible* (Ahamm means Ham, Hamma, and Black), Hastings, Vol. 2, p. 289. 1911; *Enciclopedia Universal Sopena* (Nego means Negus), Tomo Sexto, Vol. 6, p. 5947. 1964; *Unger's Bible Dictionary* (Nego means God: see Abednego), p. 2. 1957; *Jewish Family Names* (see Nebo), H. Guggenheimer, p. 340. 1992; *Grande Dicionario Etimologico-Prosodico Da Lingua Portuguesa* (Nego means Negar), Vol. 6, p. 2604. 1966; *Portuguese-English Dictionary* (Nego means Negro), J.L. Taylor, p. 440, 1970; *Concise Amharic Dictionary*, Wolf Leslau (see Negus), 1976; and *Merriam Webster's Collegiate Dictionary*

(Negus means Kings of Kings): Tenth Edition, p. 777. 1996.

89. *Egyptian Grammar* (Ng means Bull), Gardiner, p. 576. 1957; *The Pyramid Text* (Ox means Ng), Mercer, Vol. 3, p. 609. 1952; *Dr. William Smith's Dictionary of the Bible* (Am means Ham; Ham means First), Vol. 2, 986; Vol. 4, p. 3648. 1890; *A Dictionary of Urdu Classical Hindi and English* (Cow means Kam; Hamza means Alif), Platts, pp. 493, 804, 1235, pp. 1968; *Fausset's Bible Dictionary* (A means Amon), pp. 34, 269. 1971; *A Comprehensive Persian-English Dictionary* (Am and Hamzah means First and Alif), Steingass, pp. 96, 1510. 1975; *Egyptian Grammar* (Ng means Bull), Gardiner, pp. 27, 576. 1957; *Semitic Writing* (Am means Ox), Driver, pp. 54, 152. 1954; *Ala-Lc Romanization Tables* (1 and L = Alif or Hamza), 1991; *Jewish Family Names* (Kamai means First), Guggenheimer, p. 380. 1992; and *An Etymological Dictionary of Family and Christian Names* (Ham means House), Arthur, pp. 29, 152. 1857.

90. *A Comparative Grammar of the Semitic Languages* (T equal K, C and D; the T equal Th and C; the Th equal S), O'Leary, pp. 54-55, 56, 57-59, 89, 241-242. 1923; *Development of the Canaanite Dialects* (T equal H), Harris, p. 25. 1939; *On Pseudo-Corrections In Some Semitic Languages* (T equal C, D and Z), Blau, pp. 19-20, 43, 54. 1970; The letter S equal K, C and H); *A Comparative Grammar of the Semitic Languages* (S is changed to K, C and H; the S equal Th), O'Leary, pp. 56, 89, 61- 62, 221. 1923; *An Introduction to the Comparative Grammar of the Semitic Languages* (S equal H), Moscati, pp. 104, 153. 1964; *Jewish Family Names* (Chamuel), Guggenheimer, pp. 154, 397. 1992; *Materials For A Sumerian Lexicon*, Prince, p. 400. 1908; *A Comprehensive Etymological Dictionary* (Sammur means Black or Sable), Klein, Vol. 2, p. 1766. 1967; Kramers' Dutch Dictionary (Ha means Hum), Prick Van Wely, pp. 198, 811. 1946; and *The Concise Scots Dictionary* (Hum means Ham and Chew), pp. 263, 303. 1985.

91. *Diodorus, Book 3*; *The Origin of Races and Color* (Ham's children invented letters), Delany, p. 54. 1879 & 1991; *Cyclopaedia of Biblical Theological and Ecclesiastical Literature* (Ham's children invented letters), Strong, Vol. 3-4, p. 36. 1969; and *The World Book Encyclopedia*, Vol. 9, p. 224, 1994; and *Voyage en Syria et en* (Blacks invented the use of words) Egypte, Volney, Vol. 1, pp. 74-77.

92. *A Comparative Grammar of the Semitic Languages* (T equal K, C and D; the T and Th equal C; the Th equal S), O'Leary, pp. 52, 54-55, 56, 57-59, 89, 241-242. 1923; *Development of the Canaanite Dialects* (T equal H), Harris, p. 25. 1939; *On Pseudo-Corrections In Some Semitic Languages* (T equal C, D and Z), Blau, pp. 19-20, 43, 54. 1970; Egypt and Israel (T and D), Brewer, p. 301. 1910; *An Introduction to the Comparative Grammar of the Semitic Languages* (T equal H, TT and D), Moscati, pp. 29, 31, 38, 128, 153-154. 1964; *Webster's New World Hebrew Dictionary* (D equal Re), p. 534. 1992; *The World Book Encyclopedia* (Ra or Re was Egypt's Sun God); *A New System* (Ham was called the Sun and Osiris), Bryant, Vol. 1. pp. 2-5, 19, 79, 81, 104-105, 232, 250, 296-297, 340, 385; Vol. 2, pp. 130, 328, 450-451; Vol. 5, pp. 231, 247. 1807; *A Dictionary of Jewish Surnames From the Russian Empire* (The Russian Jewish H and G), Beider, pp. xv, 271. 1993; *A Commentary, Critical and Explanatory of the Old and New Testaments* (Ham was called "Amon the Sun" or "Amon-Re"), Fausset, Vol. 1, pp. 551, 700. 1870; *Religions of the World* (Re [Ra] was Osiris; Sun-God of the Nile), G.L. Berry, pp. 8-9. 1968; *The Two Babylons* (Osiris means Kamut), Hislop, pp. 23-43. 1959; Gerald Massey's Lectures (Osiris was Amen-Ra), Massey, p. 174; *A Commentary, Critical and Explanatory on the Old and New Testaments* (Ham was called Amon, Ammon, No, No-Ammon, Amon the Sun, and Populous No), Rev. Fausset, Vol. 1, pp. 551, 700. 1870; *The Holy Bible According to the Authorized Version with an Explanatory and Critical Commentary, and a Revision of Translation by*

Bishops and Other Clergy of the Anglican Church (see Nahum 3:8, No of Egypt was Ham-On), F.C. Cook, Vol. 6, 1886; *Calmet's Dictionary of The Holy Bible* (The adored Hammon or Ammon-No in Lybia and Egypt, is believed to be Ham, the son of Noah), C. Taylor, p. 448. 1833; *The Oxford English Dictionary* (see Ham), 20 Vols., 1989; *The Oxford Latin Dictionary*, p. 785. 1982-3; *A Comprehensive Etymological Dictionary* (see Hamites; Hook means Ham), Klein, Vol. 1, p. 699. 1966; *Material For a Sumerian Lexicon* (C equal I), Prince, p. x. 1908; *The Oxford English Dictionary* (see I and Cham), 20 Vols., 1989; *The Zohar* (Yod means Father), I Copy, Vol. 5, p. 406, Soncino Press, 1933; *On the Kabbalah and its Symbolism* (Yod, He, Vav and He, are the four letters of the name of God), Scholem, p. 104. 1960; *Strong's Exhaustive Concordance of the Bible* (I is called Kame and I Ama), No. 2386, 2504; *A Basic Grammar of the Ugaritic Language*, p. 189. 1984; *The Assyrian Dictionary*, Vol. 8, pp. 1, 325- 328; *The Oxford English Dictionary* (see Em, Hem, and Ham), 20 Vols., 1989; *Egypt's Place* (M equal Am), Bunsen, Book 1, p. 608. 1854; *Dr. William Smith's Dictionary of the Bible* (Am means Ham and Ammon), Vol. 4, p. 3648. 1890; *A Basic Grammar of the Ugaritic Language* (M equal Am, Amm and Im), Segert, p. 196. 1984; *Amorite Personal Names In The Mari Test* (M means Ham or Am), Huffmon, 1965: *A Compartive Grammar of the Semitic Languages* (M equal N), O'Leary, pp. 64, 77, 106. 1923; *Egyptian Hieroglyphic Dictionary* (Ni means N), Budge, Vol. 1, p. cxlviii. 1978; *Anacalypsis* (O was substituted for Ng and A), Higgins, pp. 192, 224, 229. 1836; *A Comparative Grammar of the Semitic Languages* (O equals A), O'Leary, pp. 99, 103. 1923; *Dr. William Smith's Dictionary of the Bible* (Ham means Am or Ammon), Vol. 4, p. 3648, 1890; *Sacred Books and Early Literature of The East* (Am or Amma was the Old Testament Ham), Horne, Vol. 1, p. 226. 1917; *An Egyptian Hieroglyhic Dictionary* (P means House; Re means Mouth), Budge, Vol. 1, pp. cxxvii; 415-416. 1978; *Semitic Writing* (Ra means Mouth), pp. 134. 1954; *A Commentary, Critical and*

Explanatory of the Old and New Testaments (Ham was called "Amon the Sun" or "Amon-Re"), Fausset, Vol. 1, pp. 551, 700. 1870; *An Introduction to the Comparative Grammar of the Semitic Languages* (Q equal K), pp. 38, 49, 51. 1964; *A Comparative Grammar of the Semitic Languages* (S is changed to K, C and H), O'Leary, pp. 56, 89, 61- 62, 221. 1923; *A New System* (Ham, the Deity), Bryant, Vol. 1, p. 296. 1807; Vol. 5, pp. 264-265; *A Comparative Grammar of the Semitic Languages* (T = K, C and D), O'Leary, pp. 52, 54-55, 56, 57- 59, 89, 242. 1923; *The Gods of The Egyptians*, Budge, Vol. 1, pp. 148, 334; Vol. 2, 139, 330. 1969; *Development of the Canaanite Dialects* (T = H), Harris, p. 25. 1939; *A New System,* Bryant (I Am-Us), Vol. 1, pp. 320-322. 1807; *The Oxford Latin Dictionary*, p. 785. 1982 & 1983: *The Oxford Hindi-English Dictionary* (see Kham), p. 229. 1993; *Dictionary of Word Origin* (Ham means Bend), p. 272. 1991; *On the Kabbalah and its Symbolism* (The letter Vav (V) is one of the four Hebrew letters of the name of God), Scholem, p. 104. 1960; and *A Comprehensive Etymological Dictionary* (see Hamites; Hook means Ham), Klein, Vol. 1, p. 699. 1966 and An Introduction to the *Comparative Grammar of the Semitic Languages*, (S = H, where- as the S = Z), Moscati, pp. 35, 104, 153. 1964. *The two Babylons* (X means Ham), Hislop, p. 204. 1959.

93. *Sex and Race*, Rogers, Vol. 1, 2, 3; and *Nature Knows No Color-Line*, Rogers, pp. 191-203. 1952.

94. *The King James Version* (not the new, published in 1979), Deut. 1:17; 16:19; II Chron. 19:7; Pro. 24:23; 28:21; Acts 10: 34; Ro. 2:11; Eph. 6:9; Col. 3:25; I Peter 1:17.

95. Ibid. Matt. 24:14; 28:20; John 8:32.

96. Ibid. Job 13:2.

97. *The Earth and Its Inhabitants.* Africa-, Reclus, Vol. 1, 207; *Wonderful Ethiopians of the Ancient Cushite Empire*, Houston, pp. 54, 79, 122, 150, 218. 1985; *A New System* (The Greek philosophers Solon, Thales, Pythagoras, etc., were educated in Egypt), Vol. 4, p. 387. 1807; *The Great Initiates: and A Study of the Secret History of Religions* (cave man), Schure, p. 49. 1961; *A New System* (The Jewish historians Philo, Josephus and others, says that Greek history was largely based upon myth and speculation, that the people whom the Greeks claimed as barbarians, were the same whom the Greeks borrowed their culture from. Philo says that he obtain little intelligence from the Greeks, which compelled him to travel outside the country to find the truth), Bryant, Vol. 1, pp. 182-185, 194-97, 200-207; Vol. 5, p. 50. 1807; and *Egypt Revisited: Journal of African Civilizations* (The Greeks altered every name in Egypt (Kemit) to Greek Names), Ivan Van Sertima, p. 212. 1989; *Ancient History*, C. Rollin (Zeus was Ham), Vol. 3, pp. 217-218, 1661-1741; *A New System*, Bryant (Zeus was Ham), Vol. 1, pp. 5-6, 1807; *Nature knows No Color-Line* (Zeus was Black), Rogers, p. 31. 1952; Plutarch (Ham was called Zeus), Isis et Osiris, Vol. 2. p. 354; *The History of the World* (Hammon or Ammon was the Greek's Zeus), Waters, pp. 400-405. 1971; *Ancient History* (Ham was Jupiter and Zeus), C. Rollin, Vol. 3, pp. 217-218. 1661-1741; *Oxford Latin Dictionary* (Hammo, was also called Jupiter and Ammon, was worshiped in Egypt), p. 785. 1968; *The Origin of Races and Color* (Ham was Jupiter), Delany, pp. 37, 42, 49, 57-58, 61. 1879; *A Commentary, Critical and Explanatory, on the Old and New Testaments* (Ham means Jupiter, Amon, and Sun), Fausset, Vol. 1, pp. 551, 700. 1870; *Cyclopaedia of Biblical Theological and Esslesiastical Literature* (Ham was Jupiter), Strong, Vol. 3- 4, p. 34. 1969; *From Babylon to Timbuktu* (The Greeks changed the names of the black Gods of Egypt), Windsor, p. 58. 1986; Herodotus (Greece borrowed her culture), Beloe, Vol. 1. p. 293. 1821; *Black Athena* (the Grecian African culture), Bernal, 2 Vols., 1987; *Stolen Legacy*, James, 1976; *The Legends*

of the Jews (sacred color), Vol. 2, p. 303. 1925; *Mythology Among the Hebrews and its Historical Developement* (sacred color), Goldziher, 1967; and *Mythology of all Races*, Vol. 12, pp. 94, 97, 413.

98. *The King James Version* (not the new, published in 1979), Matt. 1:5-7; Luke 3:32; *Jewish Family Names*, Guggenheimer (Sal and Zalmon means dark skin man), pp. 652, 856. 1992; *Unger's Bible Dictionary* (See Salmon and Salma), p. 955. 1957; *The Oxford English Dictionary* (see Solomon and Salmon), 20 Vols., 1989; *A New System* (Ham was Helius and Hellen), Bryant, Vol. 4, 200-201, 206. 1807; The Black Biblical Heritage, Johnson, 1999; *The Negro is a Man* (Negro Solomon, David, Jesse, Obed, Boaz, Salmon and Rahab), pp. 9, 11, 130; and *Jones' Dictionary of The Testament Proper Names* (Ham is Helius), pp. 89, 149. 1990.

99. *Egypt's Place* (Kam [Ham] means copper and bronze), Bunsen, Book 1, p. 588. 1854; *Universal Jewish Encyclopedia* (Kam means Ham), Vol. 4, p. 5. 941; September 16, 1991 issue of the U.S. News (Early Man); May 20. 1996, issue of the *U.S. News* (First Genius); January 11, 1988, issue of *Newsweek* (The Search for Adam and Eve); *Echoes of the Old Darkland* (Ham, Cham or Kam means Black), Finch, p. 133. 1991; *An Egyptian Hieroglyphic Dictionary* (Hemt [Ham] means copper; Hemt-Kam means black copper), Budge, pp. 485-86, 1978; *The Anchor Bible Dictionary* (Ham means Hmt (Hemt)), Vol. 3, p. 32, 1992; and *A Practice Sanskrit Dictionary* (Kam-Sa means Brass), p. 60. 1954.

100. *The Book of Catholic Quotations*, Chapin, p. 602. 1956.

101. *The Oxford English Dictionary* (see Kingdom), 20 Vols.; 1989; *The Zohar* (Mah means Elohim or God), I Copy, Vol. 1, pp. 5-8, 15, Soncino Press. 1933; *An Introduction to the Comparative*

Grammar of the Semitic Languages, (S = H), Moscati, pp. 35, 104, 153. 1964.

102. *Afrikan People and European Holidays: A Mental Genocide*, Barashango, Vol. 2, p. 44. 1983; and Sepia Magazine, December 1980, p. 16.

103. *The King James Version* (not the new, published in 1979), Psalms 91:1; Acts 5:15; 13:1; Heb. 4:12; *The Oxford English Dictionary* (see Om, Him, Hom, Hem, and Shad), 20 Vols., 1989; *The Ancient Hebrew Tradition* (Ni means God), Hommel, p. 60. 1897; *Kabbalah* (Nothing), Z'ev ben Shimon Halevi, p. 5. 1979; *The Mystic Quest*, D.S. Ariel, p. 74. 1988; *Zohar* (No' Am YHVH), D.C. Matt, p. 254. 1983; *Jones' Dictionary of Old Testament Proper Names* (Ham was called El and Niger), pp. 138, 296-297. 1990; *The Ancient History of the Egyptians and Carthaginians* (The Deity Ham), Vol. 1, p. 231. 1795; Vol. 3, pp. 217-218. 1661-1741; and *Herodotus*, The Reverend William Belos (Ham the youngest of Noah was vererated), Vol. 3, p. 87. 1821.

104. *The King James Version* (not the new, published in 1979), Acts 11:26.

105. Ibid. Prov. 29:18.

106. Ibid. Dan. 7:9; 10:6; Rev. 1:14-14; 4:3.

107. *Herodotus* (Greece borrowed her culture), Beloe, Vol. 1. p. 293. 1821; *Black Athena* (the Grecian African culture), Bernal, 2 Vols., 1987; *Stolen Legacy*, James, 1976; *The Earth and Its Inhabitants*. Africa-, Reclus, Vol. 1, 207; *Wonderful Ethiopians of the Ancient Cushite Empire*, Houston, pp. 54, 79, 218. 1985; *A New System* (The Greek philosophers Solon, Thales, Pythagoras, etc., were educated in Egypt), Vol. 4, p. 387. 1807; *The Great*

Initiates: and A Study of the Secret History of Religions (cave man), Schure, p. 49. 1961; and *The Mediterranian Races* (The African European), Sergi, 1901.

108. *The King James Version* (not the new, published in 1979), Jer. 36:26 38:6; *Anacalypsis*, Higgins (Jescua Ham-Massiah or Jesus Homi-Num Salvator), Vol. 1, pp. 315-316, 328, 673. 1836; *The Dead Sea Scroll and the Bible* (Jeshuah Ham-Mashiach), Pfeiffer, p. 126. 1969; *The Two Babylons* (Iusus Homi-Num), p. 164. 1959; *The Negro is a Man*, Armistead (Ham was Black), pp. xvii, xxi, 89, 153, 1903; *Encyclopedia Judaic*a (Messiah means Ham-Ashiah), Vol. 11, p. 1407. 1971; *The Jewish Encyclopedia* (Messiah means Hamashiah), Vol. 8, p. 505. 1912; *Encyclopedia Judaica* (Ha-Ra-Ham-An and Hama-Kom, see index), 1972; *The Universal Jewish Encyclopedia* (Hama-Kom and El Rahum, see God), Vol. 5, p. 191. 1969; Duden Fremdworterbuch Hamoglobin (see Ham), Marie Dose, 5th ed., p. 297. 1990; *Strong's Exhaustive Concordance* (Haima, the blood of Christ): *Greek Dictionary: No. 129; The World Book Dictionary* (see Hem), Thorndike Barnhart; *New International Dictionary of Old Testament Theology and Exegesis* (Ham means Bread), VanGemeren, Vol. 2, p. 177. 1997; *Gesenius's Hebrew and Chaldee Lexicon to the Old Testament Scriptures* (Ham means New Baked Bread), p. 285. 1857; *Concise Amharic Dictionary* (Negus means King), Wolf Leslau, 1976; *A Comprehensive Etymological Dictionary* (see Negus), Klein; *Jones' Dictionary of Old Testament Proper Names* (Ham means Black and Niger), p. 138; 1990; *Africa's Gift to America* (Niger was pronounced nigger, not Nijer), Rogers, p. 61. 1961; *Niger Ibos* (Lordly Niger), G.T. Basden, p. 113. 1966; *Dictionary of American Regional English* (see nigger), Hall, p. 788. 1985; First Steps In Assyrian (Hama-Mu means to rule), King, p. 348. 1898; *Dr. William Smith's Dictionary of the Bible* (Ham), Vol. 1, p. 4. 1890; *Enciclopedia Universal Sopena* (Nego means Negus), Tomo Sexto, Vol. 6, p. 5947. 1964; *The Oxford English Dictionary*

(Negus means King), 20 Vols., 1989; *Unger's Bible Dictionary* (Nego means God: see Abednego), p. 2. 1957; *Jewish Family Names* (see Nebo), H. Guggenheimer, p. 340. 1992; *Grande Dicionario Etimologico-Prosodico Da Lingua Portuguesa* (Nego means Negar), Vol. 6, p. 2604. 1966; *Portuguese-English Dictionary* (Nego means Negro), J.L. Taylor, p. 440, 1970; *The Oxford English Dictionary* (see letter I, C, Ch and Cham), 20 Vols., 1989; Vols., 1989; *The Black Biblical Heritage* (Blacks in the Bible), Johnson, 1999; *An Introduction To The Comparative Grammar of the Semitic Languages* (H = K, Q and G), Moscati, pp. 38-39, 52. 1964; *For A Sumerian Lexicon* (C = I), Prince, p. x. 1908; *Hebrew Union College Annual: Table 1 & 3 Narrow and Broad Romanizations* (H = HH, C, Ch, X and Zero), Vol. 40-41, 1969 & 1970; *Hebrew Union College Annual: The Old West Semitic Sun God Hammu* (Ham was worshiped by the Semites), Vol. 18, pp. 473-480. 1944; Vol. 23, p. 373. 1950 & 1956; *Merriam Webster's Collegiates Dictionary* (Negus means King of Kings), Tenth Edition, p. 777. 1996; *Dr. William Smith's of the Bible* (Ham means Am or Ammon), Vol. 4, p. 3648. 1890; *Echoes of the Old Darkland* (Ham, Cham or Kam means Black), p. 133. 1991; and *Sacred Books and Early Literature of the East* (Am or Amma was the Old Testament Ham), Horne, Vol. 1, p. 226. 1917.

109. *The King James Version* (not the new, published in 1979), Ruth 4:21-22; Matt. 1:5-7; and *The Negro is a Man* (Rahab was a Negro woman; Boaz, Obed, Jesus, David, and Solomon were colored men), pp. 9, 11, 130. 1903; and *From Babylon to Timbuktu*, Windsor, 1986. 1988. *Bible Defence of Slavery* (Jezebel was called a Negress), Josiah Priest, p. 187-88, 1853.

110. *A Commentary, Critical and Explanatory, on the Old and New Testaments* (Amen means Amen-Re, Amon and Ham), Fausset, Vol. 1, pp. 551, 700. 1870; *Oxford English Dictionary* (Hamy-Ne means Amen), 20 Vols., 1989; *The African Origin of*

Civilization (Amon means Kham), Diop, p. 149. 1974; *Sanskrit-English Dictionary* (Am or Om means Amen), Williams, p. 235. 1899; *A New System* (Ham means Amon), Bryant, Vol. 1, p. 3. 1807. *Fausset's Bible Dictionary* (Ham means Amen, Amon, Aman and Hamon), pp. 34, 269, 513. 1961; *Calmet's Dictionary of the Holy Bible* (Ammon means Hammon), p. 55. 1849; *Dr. William Smith's Dictionary of the Bible* (Ham means Am or Ammon), Vol. 4, p. 3648, 1890; *Sacred Books and Early Literature of the East* (Am or Amma was the Old Testament Ham), Horne, Vol. 1, p. 226. 1917; *In Hebrew Proper Names* (Am and Ammi are proper terms of a God), G.B. Gray, pp. 52, 44. 1896; *Biblia Sacra Polyglotta Bible*, Walton, 1654 & 1963; *Funk & Wagnalls Standard Family Dictionary* (Amen means Ammon, Amon and Amen-Re, the same as Jesus and Egypt's Sun-God), Vol. 1, p. 39. 1961; and *Hexaglot Bible.*

111. *The King James Version* (not the new, published in 1979), Job 42:14; *An Introduction to the Comparative Grammar of the Semitic Languages* (H = K, Q, G and T), Moscati, pp. 29, 31, 38-39, 52. 1964; *A Comparative Grammar of The Semitic Languages* (T = K, C and D), O'Leary, pp. 52, 54-55, 56, 57-59, 89, 242. 1923; *Development of The Canaanite Dialects* (T = H), Harris, p. 25. 1939; *On Pseudo-Corrections In Some Semitic Languages* (T = C, D and Z), Blau, pp. 19-20, 43, 54. 1970; and *Jones' Dictionary to Old Testament Proper Names* (Ham is also spelled Hham), p. 138. 1990.

112. *Encyclopedia of Religion and Ethics* (Adam was called Adham), Vol. 1, p. 84. 1908; *The Beginning of History* (Adamu means Black), Lenormant, pp. 310-314. 1899; *A New System* (Adham means Ham and Lord Ham), Bryant, Vol. 1, pp. 30, 69; Vol. 4, p. 267. 1807; *A Comprehensive Persian-English Dictionary* (Adam means brown, dusty, tawny and mulatto; Adham means Black), Steingass, pp. 29-30. 1975; *Jones' Dictionary of Old Testament Proper Names* (Adham means Lord

Ham), p. 91, 138. 1990; *Ugaritic Manual* (Ad means Father and Lord), Gordon, p. 47. 1955; *Hebrew English Lexicon* (Adam was reddish brown): *The Hebrew and Chaldee words in the Old Testament Scriptures with their Meaning in English*, p. 4, Bagster & Sons; Assyrian Dictionary (Adamatu means black blood), pt. 1, p. 95. 1964; *Hebrew Union College Annual* (Ham was Lord Hammon), Vol. 18, p. 474. 1944; *The Negro Is A Man*, Armistead, p. 3. 1903; *Encyclopedia Judaica* (Adamatu, the same as Adam means black blood), Vol. 1. p. 235. 1971; and *The Oxford English Dictionary* (Ham means Am), 20 Vols., 1989.

113. *Ethiopia and the Missing Link in African History* (Jefferson Davis), Means, p. 2. 1980; and *Children of Ham: Freed Slaves and Fugitive Slaves on the Kenya Coast 1973 to 1907*, Morton, 1990.

114. *Original African Heritage Study Bible*, The James C. Winston Publishing Company, p. 103. 1993; and *Afrikan People and European Holidays: A Mental Genocide*, Barashango, Vol. 2, p. 9. 1983.

115. *Outpouring*, Hickey (Ham, the father of Indians), Hickey, Nov., Vol. 15, No. 11, 1992: P.O. Box 17340, Denver, Co. 80111; *History of the Indian Tribes of the United States* (Indians are from Ham), Schoolcraft, Vol. 3, pp. 476-477. 1851; *Anacalypsis*, Higgins (Negroes first settled India; Indus represented blue-black. Herodotus called the Oriental Ethiopian Indians; the Greeks during Homer's age called the Indians Eastern Ethiopians), Vol. 1, pp. 54-55, 58-59, 357, 458, 631. 1836; *Cyclopeadia of India*, Balfour (Ind, India or Hindus means Black, Indian or Ethiopia; there were Negroes living India), Vol. 2, pp. 56, 151, 1073-1080. 1967; *Sanskrit-English Dictionary* (Him means Hin), p. 1298, 1899; Hobson-Jobson (The British called the people of India, "Nigger Indians"), Yule and Burnell, p. 625. 1968; *A New System*, Bryant (The Ethiopians were the original

Indi), Vol. 4, pp. 269-278, 280. 1807; *The Century Cyclopedia of Names Smith* (India means Ind and Indi), p. 526. 1914; *Calmet's Dictionary of the Holy Bible* (Hind, the son of Ham), Taylor, p. 448. 1849; *Ethiopia and The Missing Link* (India means Ethiopia), Means, p. 71, 1980; *Cyclopaedia of Biblical Theological and Ecclesiastical Literature* (Ham's children were called Indians), Strong, Vol. 3-4, p. 36. 1969; *Black Africans and Natives Americans* (The terms Negro, Negi, Colored, and Black are used for Indians), pp. 68-71, 73, 91, 191, 263; *Volney's New Researches Ancient History* (Ethiopia was called India; the Persians called the Ethiopians, "Hinds" and "Hindoos"), C.F. Volney, pp. 36, 175. 1856; *An Introduction to the Comparative Grammar of the Semitic Languages* (H = K, Q and G), Moscati, pp. 38-39, 52. 1964; *A Comparative Grammar of the Semitic Languages* (K = Kh, H, G and S), O'Leary, pp. 52, 61-62. 1923; *A New System* (Ham was Am-On, and was called the Sun and Osiris), Bryant, Vol. 1, pp. 2-5, 19, 79, 81, 104-105, 232, 250, 296-197, 340, 385; Vol. 2, pp. 130, 328, 450-451; Vol. 5, pp. 231, 247. 1807; *A Commentary, Critical and Explanatory, on the Old and New Testaments* (Multitude means Ham), Fausset, Vol. 1, pp. 551, 700. 1870; *Jones' Dictionary of Old Testament Proper Names* (Ham means Multitude), p. 138. 1990; *Dr. William Smith's Dictionary of the Bible* (Ham means Am or Ammon), Vol. 4, p. 3648, 1890; *A Complete Pocket Hebrew-English Dictionary of the Old Testament*, Feyerabend, pp. 78, 250. 1931; *Sacred Books and Early Literature of the East* (Am or Amma was the Old Testament Ham), Horne, Vol. 1, p. 226. 1917; *The World Book Encyclopedia* (Ra or Re was Egypt's Sun God); *Commentary, Critical and Explanatory of the Old and New Testaments* (Ham was called "Amon the Sun" or "Amon-Re"), Fausset, Vol. 1, pp. 551, 700. 1870; *Religions of the World* (Re was Osiris; Sun-God of the Nile), G.L. Berry, pp. 8-9, 1968; *The Two Babylons* (Osiris means Kamut), Hislop, pp. 23-43. 1959; *Gerald Massey's Lectures* (Osiris was Amen-Ra), Massey, p. 174; *Dictionary of Proper Names and Places in the Bible*, 1981;

Fausset's Bible Dictionary (Ra, a Babylonian Deity), pp. 66, 511. 1961; and *Echoes of the Old Darkland* (Ra of Nubia or Ethiopia), Finch, p. 139. 1991; *A Comparative Grammar of the Semitic Languages* (Ka means Ki, Ke, Kama or Kima), O'Leary, p. 270. 1923; *Mathews' Chinese-English Dictionary* (Ha means Ka and Black), p. 298. 1969; *Assyrian Dictionary* (Ka is pronounced Kiam, Kem, Kamma and Kam), Vol. 8, pp. 1, 108, 325. 1971; *Dongolese Nubian Lexicon* (Ka means Home), Armbruster, p. 114. 1965; *American Antiquities* (American Indians), Priest; *Origin of the American Indian* (Indians from Ham), Huddleston, pp. 37-38. 1967; and *The Oxford English Dictionary* (Home means Hame and Ham), 20 Vols., 1989.

116. *Images of Moses,* Rabbi Silver, p. 5-6. 1982; Sale (Black Moses), Al Koran, pp. 128, 257. 1784; *The Preaching of Islam,* p. 106, T.W. Arnold, Westminister, 1896; *The Negro is a Man,* Armistead, p. 8, 1903; *Jewish Family Names and their Origin* (Moses, Neger, Mor, or Moor), Guggenheimer, pp. 174, 523, 526, 529, 544, 1992; *History of Christian Names* (Mor means great), Vol. 2, pp. 11, 112. 1863; and *Nature Knows No Color-Line,* Rogers, pp. 71-77. 1952.

117. *Jewish Family Names*, Guggenheimer, pp. 152, 249, 315, 357, 526, 842. 1992; Theological Lexicon of the Old Testament (Is means Man), Westermann, Vol. 1, p. 98, 1997; *A Comprehensive Persian English Dictionary* (Ham is called Yam), Steingass, p. 1527. 1975; *The Oxford Dictionary of English Christian Names* (James means Hamish), Wilhycombe, pp. 144, 171, 1977; *History of Christian Names* (Hamish means James, Jim, and Jacob), Yonge, Vol. 1, p. 57, 1863; *Jones' Dictionary of Old Testament Proper Names* (Ham was called Or and El), pp. 296-97, 1990; *Dr. William Smith's Dictionary of the Bible* (see Ass and Hamor), 1890; and *The Concise Scots Dictionary* (As equal Ass and Is), pp. 17-18. 1985.

118. *Jewish Family Names* (Noah means Haim and Chaim), Guggenheimer, pp. 315, 504, 552; *The Negro is a Man* (Ham means Black), Armistead, pp. xiii-xiv, xx, xxii, 8, 102-103, 105, 128-129, 531, 525. 1903; and *Jones' Dictionary of Old Testament Proper Names* (Ham means Black and Niger), p. 138, 1990.

119. *Jewish Family Names*, Guggenheimer, pp. 340, 364, 544, 1992; *Egypt In the Neolithic and Archaic Periods* (No, Ni, and Nut means No-Amon and Nut-Amen), Budge, Vol. 1-2, p. 178. 1968; *A Commentary, Critical and Explanatory, on the Old and New Testaments* (Ham means Amon, Jupiter, Amon-Re, Ammon, No, No-Amon, Amon the Sun, Thebes, Diospolis or Nourisher), Fausset, Vol. 1, pp. 551, 700. 1870; and *Jones' Dictionary of Old Testament Proper Names* (Ham was called No), p. 279. 1990.

120. *Strong's Exhaustive Concordance: Greek Dictionary: No. 109;* New Thorndike Barnhart: *The World Book Dictionary* (A Hot wind called Kham-Sin, Ham-Sin or Hams-In), p. 1152. 1991; *A Dictionary Hindustani and English* (Cham relating to Air; Yam means Sea and Ocean), Forbes, pp. 327, 800, 1866; *A Comprehensive Persian-English Dictionary* (Cham, Ham, Hama or Yam means Air; Yam means Ham), Steingass, pp. 398-399, 409, 1507, 1527, 1975; *The Oxford English Dictionary* (Kamil-Kaze means Divine Wind; Or means Air), 20 Vols., 1989; Semitic Writing (Am means Ox), Driver, p. 1954; *Dr. William Smith's Dictionary of the Bible* (Am and Ham), Vol. 4, p. 3648, 1890; *Sacred Books and Early Literature of the East* (Am or Amma was the Old Testament Ham), Horne, Vol. 1, p. 226. 1817; *Unger's Bible Dictionary* (Khamseen, intense heat: see Jewish Calendar), p. 164. 1957; *The Pyramid Text* (Ox means Ng), Mercer, Vol. 3, p. 609, 1952; Duden Fremdworterbuch Hamoglobin (see Ham), Marie Dose, 5th ed., p. 297. 1990; *Strong's Exhaustive Concordance: Greek Dictionary* (Haima means the blood of Christ): No. 129; *The Thorndike Barnhart*

New International Dictionary of Old Testament Theology and Exegesis (Ham means Bread), VanGemeren, Vol. 2, p. 177. 1997; and *Gesenius's Hebrew and Chaldee Lexicon to the Old Testament Scriptures* (Ham means New Baked Bread), p. 285. 1857.

121. *Encyclopedia of Gods* (Col means the Black God of the rain), Jordan, 1993; Dongolese Nubian Lexicon (see Or), Armbruster. 1965; *Jones' Dictionary of Old Testament Proper Names* (Ham was called Or and El), pp. 296-297.

122. *Gesenius's Hebrew and Chaldee Lexicon to the Old Testament Scriptures* (Hachaliah), Wilhelm, pp. 276, 278, 724. 1857.

123. *A Dictionary of Jewish Surnames From the Russian Empire*, Beider, pp. xv, 271.

124. *The King James Version* (not the new, published in 1979), Deut. 32:7; Rev. 1:19.

125. *The New Funk and Wagnalls Encyclopedia* (the earliest Babylonians were a non-Semitic Negritic people), Vol. 12, pp. 4199-4200; *Dr. William Smith's Dictionary of The Bible* (The Hamitic Chaldean), Vol. 2, p. 1735. 1890; *The Ancient World* (the Babylonians were Hamites), Betten, p. 3, 1942; *Sex and Race* (Herodotus), p. 59, 1968; *The Semites in Ancient History* (The Assyrians, Babylonian, Hebrews, and Arabs were of one people), Moscati, p. 15, 1959; *The Family Bible* (Ashur Means Black), Avenel Books, 1958; *Gesenius's Hebrew and Chaldee Lexicon to the Old Testament Scriptures* (Ashur means Black), p. 85. 1857; and *Anacalypsis* (The Chaldees were Negroes), Higgins, Vol. 2, p. 364. 1836.

126. *The King James Version* (not the new, published in 1979), Judg. 4:2, 13, 16.

127. *Outpouring*, Hickey, Nov., Vol. 15, No. 11, 1992: P.O. Box 17340, Denver, Co. 80111; and *Great African Thinkers* (The Canaanites were originally Negroes), Ivan Van Sertima, Vol. 1, p. 123. 1986. *Bible Defence of Slavery*, (Professor Diop and Josiah Priest called the Canaanites Negroes) Josiah Priest, 1853.

128. *Dongolese Nubian Lexicon* (Ar means King), Armbruster, p. 163. 1965; *Oxford English Dictionary* (see Or, Ar and Ur) 20 Vols., 1989; *Jones' Dictionary of Old Testament Proper Names* (Ham was called El and Or), pp. 296-297. 1990; A New System, Bryant (Ham was called Ham-Ur and Ham-Ar), Vol. 1, p. 3. 1807; *A New System* (Ham was called El and Or), Bryant, Vol. 1, p. 89. 1979; and Brugsch's *Egypt Under the Pharaohs* (Ur and Uru means King), Vol. 2, p. 285. 1881.

129. *International Bible Dictionary* (Ham, the father of Cush, Mizraim, Phut, Canaan, and the Africans in general, was burnt-swarthy black), p. 182, Logos International, Plainfield, New Jersey, 1977; *Encyclopedia Judaica* (Cush or Cushi in Hebrew means Negro), Vol. 5, p. 1174. 1971; *Peloubet's Bible Dictionary* (Ham is defined as Black), Grand Papids, Mich., Zondervan Publishing House; *Outpouring* (Ham and Cush means Black; Phut or Libya meant Black), Hickey, Nov., Vol. 15, No. 11, 1992: P.O. Box 17340, Denver, Co. 80111; *Blacks in Antiquity* (Black Kush or Ethiopians), Snowden, 1970; *The African Origin of Civilization* (Egypt, a Negro Nation), pp. ix, xiv. 1974; and *Young's Analytical Concordance to the Bible* (Kem or Egypt is equivalent to Ham, meaning Black and warm. Ham also means swarthy-dark colored), p. 443. 1982; *The Negro is a Man* (Ham is called Black and Negro), Armistead, pp. xiii-xiv, xx, xxii, 8, 102-103, 105, 128-129, 531, 1903; *The New American Bible* (The issue concerning Ham and Canaan offers no justification for

enslaving Negroes, even though Canaan was a son of Ham), p. 14, 1970; *The Message Magazine* (The origin of the Negro is traced to Ham), Vol. 40, No. 6, September, 1974, Southern Association, Box 59, Nashville, Tennessee 37202; and *Harper's Bible Dictionary* (Ham's is believed to be the ancestor of Africans as his brother Shem was of the Semites and Japheth of the Europeans), Miller, p. 242, 1952.

130. *The King James Version* (not the new, published in 1979), Pro. 20:13 Isa. 33:6.